# CATALYST 2
## Writing from Reading

**MARIANNE BREMS**
*Mission College*

**STEVE JONES**
*Series Editor, Community College of Philadelphia*

D1441695

Australia • Canada • Mexico • Singapore • Spain • United Kingdom • United States

**THOMSON**
TM
**HEINLE**

**Catalyst: Writing from Reading 2**
*Marianne Brems and Steve Jones*

**Publisher:** *Sherrise Roehr*
**Acquisitions Editor:** *Tom Jefferies*
**Director of Product Development:** *Anita Raducanu*
**Director of Product Marketing:** *Amy Mabley*
**Executive Marketing Manager:** *Jim McDonough*
**Associate Production Editor:** *John Sarantakis*
**Manufacturing Manager:** *Marcia Locke*

**Production Project Manager:** *Cindy Johnson*
**Photo Researcher:** *Vickie Piercey*
**Cover Designer:** *Gina Petti*
**Index:** *Alexandra Nickerson*
**Composition:** *Publishing Services*
**Printer:** *Edwards Brothers*

**Cover Image:** Getty Images

For more information, contact Thomson Heinle, 25 Thomson Place, Boston, MA 02210 USA, or visit our Internet site at elt.thomson.com.

ISBN-13: 978-0-6185-4974-0
ISBN-10: 0-6185-4974-9

ISE ISBN-13: 978-1-4240-1735-5
ISE ISBN-10: 1-4240-1735-1

Library of Congress Control Number: 2007923314

**Text Credits:** Copyrights and credits appear on pages 223–224, which constitute an extension of the copyright page.

**Photo Credits:** Page 1: Bruce Laurance/Getty Images; page 2: © Matthias Kulka/zefa/CORBIS; page 12: © Ted Aljibe/AFP/Getty Images; page 29: © Joel W. Rogers/CORBIS; page 30: © Comstock/SuperStock; page 39: © David McNew/Getty Images; page 47: © Hulton Archive/Getty Images; page 53: © Pictorial Parade/Getty Images; page 54: © Jacques Langevin/CORBIS SYGMA; page 64: © Wolfgang Kaehler/CORBIS; page 72: © Bettmann/CORBIS; page 73: © Wallace Kirkland/Getty Images; page 81: © Bob Krist/CORBIS; page 82: © age/fotostock/SuperStock; page 92: © Tim McGuire/CORBIS; page 102: © Craig Lovell/CORBIS; page 109: © Image Source Pink/Getty Images; page 110: © Nicholas Prior/Getty Images; page 121: © Greer & Associates/SuperStock; page 125: © Nicholas Prior/Getty Images; page 133: © Steve Raymer/CORBIS; page 134: © Jose Luis Pelaez Inc./Getty Images; page 143: © Masterfile; page 148: © Peter Kuper 2007; page 157: © Reuters/CORBIS; page 158: © Art Shay/Time & Life Pictures/Getty Images; page 167: © Christophe Calais/CORBIS; page 173: © Bettmann/CORBIS; page 185: © Michael Goldman/Masterfile; page 186: © Dawn Hudson/istockphoto.

# Contents

# Chapter 8: American Values    185

# Introduction

## The Catalyst Series

*Catalyst* is a two-book writing series that fills a specific need for high-beginning to low-intermediate-level ESL composition students in college, university, or adult education programs. The authors developed these materials for use in their own community college programs because they were looking for academically-oriented material that was simultaneously sophisticated in its content, well-grounded in the best second-language pedagogy, and yet comparatively low in its language level. They used versions of these materials for some time in their own writing classes and, based on their positive experiences with them, they wanted to share them with the wider world of English language teaching.

The key aspects of the *Catalyst* series are:

**Content** All of the material in the books centers on the experiences of immigrants to the United States and makes connections from those experiences to academic disciplines. The chapter topics deal with goals and issues that the authors have become familiar with while teaching college ESL. Students are more engaged in their writing when they are asked to write about topics that relate to their everyday lives (and dream lives!), and this engagement results in more learning. Although the focus is on urban, working-class students, students with other experiences and situations, including international students, will certainly benefit from these materials as well.

**Vocabulary** The reading sections in the series include the study of vocabulary. There is a special emphasis on groups of words that appear in the Academic Word List. This frequently-encountered academic vocabulary is studied and practiced with an eye toward future work in college courses in all fields.

**Pedagogy** The *Catalyst* series is somewhere between the traditional "rhetorical structures/grammar" and "strong process" approaches to teaching. Both approaches have good points, so it's wise to combine them pragmatically. The organization of a written piece is taught in a traditionally explicit manner, and students are expected to understand concepts such as topic, topic sentence, introduction, etc., and to impose those concepts on their writing. However, learning happens only when a context creates a need for a new concept or structure. Writing for a purpose comes first, and organizational and grammatical tinkering come second. Students benefit from specific guidance about the particulars of writing, but some of the deepest learning is done inductively. This considered mixture of approaches is reflected in the *Catalyst* series.

In these books, reading selections play a prominent role. Compelling readings at the appropriate level help students to become more engaged in their learning, and they also give students a chance to learn both inductively and consciously about the features they are studying. The readings serve as a "catalyst" to stimulate a reaction in writing from students. They will respond with their own thoughts about topics significant to them that they want to get on paper.

The integration of the grammatical and organizational points is very carefully managed within the process of writing. Students are first asked to *find and recognize* important features in examples of writing. Then they are asked to write on related topics, concentrating on meaning, rather than form. It is in the rewriting stage, when most of the issues of meaning have been dealt with, that students are asked to focus fully on the rhetorical and grammatical topics they have studied and practiced.

Writing assignments in this series generally ask students to write more than one paragraph. We believe that beginning students can benefit from the study of basic ideas about the organization of written works, which are often left for more advanced materials.

In addition to the first two readings in each chapter in the series, which are mostly personal narratives, the third readings are designed to introduce students to a more academic prose style. These academic readings may be at a level that is a step above that of the students, but they are designed to remain accessible. First, they are supported by graphic information, including photographs, charts, and maps. Second, the language is challenging but controlled.

Teachers are invited to ask their students to read the following introduction to this volume in the *Catalyst* series. It outlines the key components of each chapter and gives a brief explanation of how the series links reading, composing, and the study of vocabulary and grammar.

# To the Student

*Catalyst*, the title of this book, means "something that accelerates a change." We hope this book will help you speed up improvement in your writing because your interest in the reading topics will give you ideas you want to write about. Readings in the book are based on the experiences of other students like you who came to the United States and now live in a new country with different customs and problems.

*Catalyst 2* is an intermediate-level composition text for students who plan to take college-level courses, so they need to learn college writing skills while they learn English grammar, vocabulary, and composition. In this book, you will discuss and react to a rich selection of readings that are designed to act as a catalyst to learning writing skills and strategies. The text is designed for students who want more practice using English in academic settings.

Each chapter has the same sections. The skills you will practice in each section are consistent throughout the chapters. These are the sections in each chapter:

**Exploring the Topic** This section will help you to focus your thoughts on the topic. It will also help you remember what you already know or think about this topic. In addition, it summarizes important points about the topic so you know what to expect as you continue through the chapter.

**Reading 1** Each chapter begins with a reading that introduces the topic of the chapter. This reading is usually about the personal experiences of one or more people. It gives you a first-hand account of how real people deal with some particular aspect of immigrant life.

**Discussion** Discussion is an important part of the writing process. When you put your thoughts into words to talk about them, it helps you clarify your ideas. Also, when other people respond to what you say, it often gives you new ideas. All of this can be helpful to you when you begin developing a composition on the topic.

**Vocabulary** A study of the academic vocabulary words from the reading is useful for comprehension as well as for expressing your ideas about the topic. These are words that you will continue to encounter and use in your academic course work.

**Composition Analysis** In this section you will study the ways that writers organize and present ideas in a composition. When you study how other writers put ideas together, you will learn about how to organize your own writing.

**Writing 1** In this section, you will first discuss a few questions about your topic with a partner. This will help you think about what you want to say. Afterwards, you may write your opinion about the topic based on your analysis of Reading 1, or you may write about a personal experience related to the topic. Writing 1 contains a choice of at least two topics. Your teacher may choose one of these topics for you, or she may ask you to choose one yourself.

**Grammar**  In this section, you will study a grammar topic that comes from examples in Reading 1. A brief explanation of this grammar point will help you understand the examples so that you can use these structures in the activities more effectively. These grammar topics will particularly help you express your ideas more clearly in the composition assignments for each chapter.

**Rewriting 1**  An important part of the writing process is for you to review your writing to learn to make it better. In this book, the first part of the review, the **Peer Activity**, comes from the suggestions of your partner and your own review of these suggestions. The second part comes from your review of your teacher's comments on the **Composition Evaluation Sheet** from Appendix 1. Then you will refer to a **Checklist** of points about content, organization, and grammar that your composition should include. Finally, you will rewrite your composition to make it clearer and more meaningful.

**Reading 2**  Reading 2 continues the development of the topic introduced in Reading 1. It gives you a chance to think about the topic more deeply and to further explore your own ideas about it. In some chapters, Reading 2 is a continuation of Reading 1.

**Discussion**  As part of the discussion activity for Reading 2, a **Group Activity** provides an opportunity for you to examine the topic as a group. You have a task to complete or a problem to solve together.

**Making Connections**  This section explores ways that Reading 1 and Reading 2 are related. In looking for these connections, you will discover new meaning and gain further understanding of the topic.

**Reading 3**  This is an academic reading that continues with the same topic as Readings 1 and 2. In addition, it provides a model of the kind of academic essay you will write in Writing 2. Because its main function is as a model of an essay format, no vocabulary study follows this reading.

**Composition Analysis**  This section explains the purpose of the kind of academic essay presented in Reading 3. It also provides practice with the concepts in the explanation.

**Writing 2**  In this section, you may write your opinion about the topic based on your analysis of one or more of the readings, or, as in Writing 1, you may write about a personal experience related to the topic. In Writing 2, however, you will write a particular kind of composition, for example, a narrative essay. As in Writing 1, Writing 2 has a choice of at least two topics. Your teacher may choose one of these topics for you, or she may ask you to choose one yourself.

# To the Teacher

*Catalyst 2* is an intermediate-level academically-oriented ESL writing text.

The text is "academic" in the sense that the chapters cover a range of academic disciplines. The readings provide a wide variety of rich, thematically-based content that serves as the catalyst for thoughtful student writing. Writing assignments ask students to analyze and react to the academic articles they have read. At the same time, vocabulary and grammatical structures at the appropriate level are presented. We have taken particular care with the level of the readings to balance interest, an academic focus, and a language level appropriate for intermediate-level students.

The vocabulary in each reading has been analyzed for its frequency of appearance in general English, and also for its appearance in the Academic Word List. The main vocabulary focus is on words from this Academic Word List. Less common words, when they appear, are glossed for students in footnotes.

The grammatical features drawn from the readings are as follows:

- Choosing the correct form—gerund or infinitive
- Uses of modal auxiliaries—*can, could, should, may,* and *must*
- Choosing the correct verb tense—simple past tense or present perfect
- Uses of passive sentences
- Uses of different transition words and phrases
- Choosing the correct verb tense—past progressive or past perfect
- Using contrast and comparison words
- Uses of factual conditional sentences
- How to avoid run-on sentences
- Choosing the correct verb tense—present perfect or past perfect
- Avoiding sentence fragments
- Maintaining parallel structure
- Correct use of adjective clauses
- Repetition of words and patterns for emphasis and cohesion
- Maintaining verb tense consistency

*Catalyst 2* focuses on compositions of more than one paragraph. This gives students freedom beyond the confines of a paragraph to explore their ideas. In addition, it gives students exposure to the concepts of an introductory paragraph, body paragraphs, and a conclusion. The kinds of essays presented are:

- A cause and effect essay
- A narrative essay
- A descriptive essay
- A comparison/contrast essay
- An argument essay
- A definition essay
- A process essay
- An evaluation essay

# Acknowledgments

First, I wish to express my gratitude to Kathy Sands Boehmer, whose expertise and patience have been instrumental for me, and to Annamarie Rice, Evangeline Bermas, and Joann Kozyrev, who have handled countless details big and small behind the scenes. I also wish to thank Cindy Johnson for her expert and meticulous copyediting and layout.

Next, my thanks go to my personal team:

Steve Jones, *Catalyst* series editor, whose editorial comments and enthusiasm for this project have been critical

Emily Strauss, a colleague, who advised me when I needed it and wrote the article, "A Land of Diversity," which appears in Chapter 2

Joan Bresnan, my partner and renowned linguistics professor, who patiently answered dozens of linguistic questions concerning style, usage, and grammar

Marsha Chan, a colleague, who led me to conceive this project by recommending me as a reviewer for *Catalyst 1*

My mother, the first immigrant in my life, who asked with interest to read my entire manuscript because of her own experiences as an immigrant

Others who deserve credit are the reviewers of the *Catalyst 2* manuscript:

Edina Bagley, *Nassau Community College*
Eric Bohman, *William R. Harper College*
Nancy Boyer, *Golden West College*
Quan Cao, *Palm Beach Community College*
Jennifer Castello, *Cañada College*
Keiko Kimura, *Triton College*
Jane Shea, *Quinsigamond Community College*
William Shoaf, *City College of San Francisco*
Lisa Stelle, *Northern Virginia Community College*
Elizabeth Wagenheim, *Prince George's Community College*

Marianne Brems
Santa Clara, California

# Catalyst 2: Scope and Sequence

| Chapter Topics | Reading Topics | Composition Analysis and Writing Competencies | Writing Topics | Grammar Competencies |
|---|---|---|---|---|
| **CHAPTER 1**<br>The remittance life | The lives of remittance workers<br><br>How remittances work<br><br>Remittances—a good opportunity for banks | Main ideas and supporting details<br><br>Topic sentences as predictors<br><br>A cause and effect essay | The separation of remittance life<br><br>A cause and effect essay about remittances | Gerunds and infinitives<br><br>Modal auxiliaries: *can, could, should, may, must* |
| **CHAPTER 2**<br>Discrimination | Personal experiences with discrimination<br><br>A historical account of discrimination against the Chinese<br><br>A historical account of Japanese internment | Controlling ideas and topic sentences<br><br>Using narrative accounts to support historical facts<br><br>A narrative essay | The effect of understanding on discrimination<br><br>A narrative essay about experiences with discrimination | The simple past and present perfect verb tenses<br><br>Passive sentences |
| **CHAPTER 3**<br>Bridging a gap through athletics | The Bering Strait swim (Part 1)<br><br>The Bering Strait swim (Part 2)<br><br>Breaking barriers through athletics | Thesis statements in essays<br><br>Transitions showing time<br><br>A descriptive essay | Facing challenges to achieve success<br><br>A descriptive essay about bridging a gap through athletics | Transition words and phrases<br><br>The past progressive and past perfect verb tenses |
| **CHAPTER 4**<br>Family issues and marriage | Keeping or breaking family tradition<br><br>Arranged marriage vs love marriage<br><br>American weddings as a reflection of American values | Conclusions in essays<br><br>Contrast and comparison words<br><br>A comparison/contrast essay | Making an important decision<br><br>A comparison/contrast essay about attitudes toward family and marriage | Contrast words and phrases<br><br>Factual conditional sentences |
| **CHAPTER 5**<br>The effects of stereotypes | Dealing with stereotypes as an Asian American<br><br>Food names as an expression of ethnic stereotypes<br><br>The difficulties of a model minority | Supporting details for opinion statements<br><br>Titles for essays<br><br>An argument essay | Stereotypes as barriers<br><br>An argument essay about the destructive effects of stereotypes | Run-on sentences<br><br>The present perfect and past perfect verb tenses |

| Chapter Topics | Reading Topics | Composition Analysis and Writing Competencies | Writing Topics | Grammar Competencies |
|---|---|---|---|---|
| **CHAPTER 6** <br> The process of assimilation | Immigrants resisting the idea of assimilation <br><br> A Norwegian discovers herself in a visit home <br><br> America is no longer the melting pot | Specific actions and general explanations used in supporting statements <br><br> Finding support sentences <br><br> A definition essay | The choices of assimilation <br><br> A definition essay about the assimilation process | Sentence fragments <br><br> Parallel structure |
| **CHAPTER 7** <br> Refugees finding a place to belong | A refugee finds a place to call home (Part 1) <br><br> A refugee finds a place to call home (Part 2) <br><br> The scientific principle of relativity | Defining levels of generality <br><br> Finding levels of generality <br><br> A process essay | First impressions of a new country <br><br> A process essay about a useful process | Adjective clauses <br><br> Repetition of key words |
| **CHAPTER 8** <br> American values | The attitudes behind American values (Part 1) <br><br> The attitudes behind American values (Part 2) <br><br> Hybrid-electric vehicles | Headings <br><br> Using "you" to connect to the reader <br><br> An evaluation essay | Exploring an American value <br><br> An evaluation essay analyzing a value | Transition words for different purposes <br><br> Verb tense consistency |

# 1 The Remittance Life

## Exploring the Topic

**Discussion** Almost as soon as immigrants began arriving in the United States, they started sending money, in the form of remittances, to relatives back home. Today, even more immigrants are working hard and sending even more dollars abroad.

In groups of 3–4, discuss the following questions. Then share your ideas with the class.

1. Have you ever left someone you wanted to be with so that you could help from a distance? How did you feel about this?

2. What do you think it does to families to be separated for long periods of time? Be specific.

3. Is separating a family to "have a better life" more important than keeping a family together? Why?

4. Do you think people who send remittance dollars to family members have a sense of pride about what they're doing? Explain your answer.

## Reading 1: Personal Experience Reading

This reading is based on the remittance lives of two young girls; Karin and Arlene. Both are strongly committed to serving their families in the best way they can. Both make what we might consider great personal sacrifices to send money home.

As you read this story, think about what each girl gains and what she loses in living the remittance life. You will use your thoughts later in this chapter.

## The Struggle to Support Faraway Families

1      A week after her high school graduation in Tegucigalpa, Honduras, Karin moved to the United States. She lives in Hialeah, a city outside Miami.[1] Hialeah is filled with Spanish-speaking immigrants, pawnshops,[2] and little diners serving *café con leche*. She shares a two-bedroom apartment with her mom, uncle, aunt, and two baby cousins. She has to hide when she sees the landlady, since she does not know Karin lives there, and bite her lip when she feels waves of homesickness.[3] She doesn't go to the movies, or make friends, or even know about nearby stylish South Beach.

2      Instead, Karin has found work and has started sending money home to her father and two brothers back in Honduras. She makes $460 a month working as a

[1] *Miami:* a large city in Florida
[2] *pawnshop:* a place where you can borrow money with personal property as security
[3] *homesickness:* a strong feeling of missing home

waitress and a baby sitter. From that, she sends $300 home through a local money-wiring service. Most of the rest of her money goes toward her share of the rent, simple necessities, and bus fare for rainy days. She often wears the same clothes for days in a row, always pushes her hair back in a simple ponytail, and never uses makeup. Last month she bought herself a pair of comfortable work shoes. This month she plans to go out to a nice meal with her aunt. She has not saved a penny.

3   Before Karin came to the United States, she burned all her childhood toys, gave away most of her clothes to her cousins, and presented her portable CD player to her dad. "The idea was to come and work—not bring stuff here," she explains. "My life ended there and now begins again."

## The Remittance Life

4   About forty-two percent of the immigrants in the United States from Latin America and the Caribbean send remittances home regularly. The total from these approximately six million legal and illegal immigrants added up to about $30 billion in 2002. For most of the recipient countries, these remittances are greater than all investment by foreigners and foreign firms. They account for more than ten percent of the gross domestic product[4] (GDP) in six of the countries. In Nicaragua, remittances are as high as thirty percent of the GDP. As immigration to the United States from that part of the world continues to grow, these numbers are also growing.

5   For some immigrants—those with more income—sending off hard-earned money every week or month is no big problem. For others, like Karin, it is a struggle. Close to half of the men and women sending remittances make less than $30,000 a year. Many of them make much less. This means that these immigrants work day in and day out[5] and live simply so that faraway parents, siblings, or children can live a little better.

6   It often works like this. A family will save money and send one or two members to the United States. Later, that person will support the larger family until a different relative arrives to join in the efforts or to take over. Most young immigrants arriving in the United States from Latin America expect to continue this process. If they grew up with homes, school fees, and food all paid for by relatives working in the United States, then they know they need to do their part.

## Family Comes First

7   Arlene is getting married. She has a little engagement ring with the date Julio asked her to marry him and a wedding date written on the inside. Julio is the only man in the world for her, she says. Yet she knows she needs to control her excitement and focus on her priorities. "My parents and brothers come first," she explains.

8   Arlene lives with her father and young brother in Key West.[6] She works at a laundromat and at a café, and sends most of her $300-a-month earnings home to her mother and other brother in Managua. Her fiancé works as a salesman at Sears in Miami where he lives with his mother. Most of his salary also goes to his father

[4] *gross domestic product:* the total value of goods and services produced by a nation (often abbreviated GDP)
[5] *day in and day out:* every day without fail
[6] *Key West:* an island which is part of the state of Florida

and sister in Managua. The young couple have very little money—or time—for each other. Despite their difficulties, neither Arlene nor Julio complains.

9    "Times were terrible when I was very young in Nicaragua," she says. "We never had meat or white sugar and our bars of soap were scratchy and enormous. Then when I was seven my father said 'Enough!' and traveled by himself to America. He went first to Mexico, then sneaked across the border to Key West. There he lived in a trailer and worked two jobs—as a cook in a hospital by day and as a restaurant dishwasher at night. He soon began sending money and packages home: a bag of toys one time, socks and T-shirts another. Every month he sent more than $500 for the family to live on. At Christmas he would send each child $50. Once every two years he would buy plane tickets and the whole family would travel to Florida. He never returned to Nicaragua, even for a visit.

10    "Now I realize that if we started to live the good life it was because of my father," says Arlene. "I studied in a private high school and learned accounting ... all thanks to him." Now her father is sick, and her mother, brother, and many aunts and cousins are struggling to live in Nicaragua. It is her turn to help.

11    "When I was a child I'd swear I would never do what my family did, separating Mom from Dad, me from my brothers. Even for the money ..." recalls Arlene. "And still, I don't want the sort of marriage my parents had." However, she admits, Julio is thinking of going to Nicaragua to take care of family while she might stay in Florida to care for her family and send money back home. "Situations come up," she says. "I always felt sorry for my mom and dad. But I will be just like them."

### Dreams Put on Hold

12    Just seventeen, Karin has needed to lie to survive her new life. She lied about her age to get her job at the diner. She lied to immigration officials about her intentions when she came into the country on a tourist visa. And she lies to the landlady about where she lives. "I wanted to come because I wanted to help my dad," she says, slowly preparing a cup of coffee for a customer in the diner.

13    Her father worked at a brewery[7] in South Florida when she was a child and sent home $200 a month to Honduras. This was just enough for her to go to school, where she studied computers. Now, Karin's father is back in Honduras with her two younger siblings, and she and her mother are expected to send the money for their school fees.

14    She had thought, perhaps, she would save money, buy an old laptop, go to night school, learn English, and do something with her training. Maybe she would become a computer engineer. Her dad warned her that her dreams were too big. She had thought she still had a chance. Now, she is not so sure. She feels sad and yet also satisfied with her life. "America is nice ... I suppose," she says. "And anyway, for me, it's just a job."

[7] *brewery:* a place where beer is made

**Discussion** Discuss these questions with your classmates.

1. Why does Karin hide when she sees the landlady? Why does she wear the same clothes for days in a row and not wear makeup? How do you think she feels about this?

2. Why do so many immigrants participate in the remittance life?

3. Do you think Arlene's parents and brothers should come before her fiancé? Why or why not?

4. Do you think Arlene's dream of becoming a computer engineer is too big? Should she listen to her father or should she follow her dream? Explain.

## Vocabulary

ACTIVITY 3

**Academic Words** Circle the letter of the definition that best matches the meaning of each **boldface** word.

1. It costs Juan **approximately** fifty dollars a month to send money home to his family in Mexico.

    a. exactly     b. about     c. nearly

2. A regular program of **investment** can be a good way to make money for the future.

    a. putting money into a company     b. working     c. spending money

3. Because I had six **siblings**, my father had to work three jobs to support us all.

    a. brothers and sisters     b. cousins     c. aunts and uncles

4. One of Ming's highest **priorities** when he left China for the United States was to gain the freedom he had heard so much about.

    a. difficulties     b. jobs     c. important desires

5. Driving in bad weather requires a great deal of **focus**.

    a. close attention     b. good vision     c. attention to detail

6. American teenagers like to wear jeans with holes in them because they think it is **stylish**.

    a. clearly not caring about money     b. fashionable     c. comfortable

7. Tuan and Diep have been **a couple** for twenty years.

    a. a pair     b. two people living in the same house     c. friends

8. For the purpose of sending remittances, the status of an immigrant's papers does not seem to matter. Legal as well as **illegal** immigrants send money to support their families back home.

   a. breaking the law     b. following the law     c. having a visa

9. One of the main reasons that immigrants come to the United States is to earn more **income** for their families.

   a. safety     b. money     c. respect

10. Immigrants often come to the United States with the **intention** of making their dreams come true.

    a. energy     b. preparation     c. purpose

## Composition Analysis

**Main Ideas and Supporting Details**  A well-written paragraph or essay is one that makes the writer's point of view clear. One way that the writer does this is by presenting general main ideas and specific details that support the point of view (the author's opinion) expressed in the main idea. We can think of the main idea as the foundation of a house and the details as the rooms. The foundation provides a structure on which to build rooms. The rooms give purpose to the foundation.

Look at how main ideas are supported by details in the following example from Reading 1. (The point of view is in **boldface**.)

Main Idea

A family will save money and send one or two members to the United States. Later, that person will support the larger family until a different relative arrives to join in the efforts or to take over. **Most young immigrants arriving in the United States from Latin America expect to continue this process.**

Supporting Details

"Now I realize that if we started to live the good life it was because of my father [working in the United States]," says Arlene. "I studied in a private high school and learned accounting ... all thanks to him." Now her father is sick, and her mother, brother, and many aunts and cousins are struggling to live in Nicaragua. It is her turn to help.

Look at the following main idea statements from the reading. Find detail statements in the reading that support them.

1. **Main Idea:** For some immigrants—those with more income—sending off hard-earned money every week or month is no big problem. For others, like Karin, it is a struggle.

    **Supporting Details:** _____

    _____

    _____

2. **Main Idea:** Just seventeen, Karin has needed to lie to survive her new life.

    **Supporting Details:** _____

    _____

    _____

3. **Main Idea:** *(find one in the reading)* _____

    _____

    _____

    **Supporting Details:** _____

    _____

    _____

# *Writing 1*

**ACTIVITY 5**  To help you prepare for the writing assignment in the next section, choose a topic below and discuss the questions with a partner who has chosen the same topic as you. Write answers to the questions in your own words. You do not need to agree with your partner as long as you can give reasons for your answers.

### Topic 1

1. Which do you think is more important, becoming a remittance worker or keeping the family together?

2. What are the gains and losses that result from your choice?

### Topic 2

1. What important experience have you had that caused you to be away from your family for a long time?

2. How did you feel about what you did?

3. How did you feel about your separation?

**ACTIVITY 6**  **Writing Assignment**  Write a composition about one of the following topics. Be sure to include in your paper all of the items in the checklist on page 11.

### Topic 1

Do you think that becoming a remittance worker is worth the pain of separating a family? Discuss the gains and losses using details from Reading 1 to support your answer.

### Topic 2

Tell about a time when you had to leave your family or a loved one for a long time to do something important. Give examples of how you felt about what you did and how you felt about your separation to support your main ideas.

# Grammar

| Gerunds and Infinitives | **Gerunds** are forms of verbs. They look like verbs because they end in *-ing*, but they do not act like verbs. They are actually nouns. They can appear in sentences in all the places that nouns appear. A gerund is formed by adding *-ing* to the base form of a verb. In Sentence 1 below, the gerund is the *subject* of the sentence. In Sentence 2, the gerund is the *object* of a verb. |
|---|---|

1 **Sending** money home from the United States is sometimes more important to an immigrant than staying with the family in her home country.
2 Instead, Karin has found work and has started **sending** money home to her father and two brothers back in Honduras.

Gerunds are used as objects after the following common verbs:

| admit | avoid | consider | continue | deny |
|---|---|---|---|---|
| enjoy | finish | miss | practice | recommend |
| resent | start | stop | suggest | understand |

Prepositions such as the following often precede gerunds:

| by | for | in | instead of | of |
|---|---|---|---|---|
| on | to | with | without | |

**Infinitives** are verbs that are formed by putting *to* before the base form of the verb. For example:

She lied about her age **to get** her job at the diner.
"The idea was **to come** and work—not bring stuff here," she explains.

Infinitives are used after certain verbs such as:

| agree | begin | decide | expect | hope |
|---|---|---|---|---|
| learn | manage | need | plan | refuse |
| seem | try | want | | |

Note that some sentences can use either a gerund or an infinitive.

**ACTIVITY 7** Choose the gerund or infinitive form of the word given to fill in each blank and complete the sentences. Some words can be used in either the gerund or the infinitive form.

Irma is about (1. graduate) _____ from high school in Mexico.

(2. study) _____ computer science at a university in the United States is her

dream. She wants (3. become) _____ a computer programmer. She is a good

student and she has good grades in math, but (4. care) _____ for the family

comes first. Irma's father went to the United States (5. work) _____ four

years ago so he could send money home for the family (6. live) _____ on.

Now, after (7. work) _____ in a factory for two years, his back hurts much of

the time. He tries (8. stay) _____ and work twelve-hour shifts, but sometimes

the pain is too much. He wants (9. continue) _____ (10. work) _____

and (11. send) _____ money home, but it is very difficult for him. Irma

thinks she needs (12. be) _____ ready (13. begin) _____ the

remittance life in his place. She knows if she does relieve him, (14. go) _____

to college will have to wait for at least a few years. She is not sure what

(15. do) _____.

**ACTIVITY 8** Find the eight gerund or infinitive errors in the paragraph below and correct them. Be careful, sometimes both a gerund and an infinitive are correct.

In many countries, such as Mexico, for example, banks are not federally insured

as in the United States. Without insurance, depositors understand it is possible

losing all their money overnight. For this reason, many Mexican nationals working

in the United States are unwilling opening bank accounts. They want seeing,

feeling, and most of all counting their cash. The result is that they often must pay

more sending remittances. First, if they receive a payroll check, they must pay

cashing it. Second, using a money-wiring service is usually more costly than

sending money home through a bank. For this reason, financial management

classes for migrant workers recommend to open bank accounts.

# Rewriting 1

ACTIVITY 9 **Peer Activity** Trade your composition from Activity 6 with another student. Read your partner's paper and underline the topic sentence of the paragraph or paragraphs <u>once</u> and the point of view statement <u>twice</u>. Decide if the details in each paragraph support each of the main ideas. Then talk to your partner about what you found and help him or her make any necessary changes.

ACTIVITY 10 **On Your Own** Review your partner's notes, your partner's comments, and your teacher's feedback on the first draft of your composition. Look at the Composition Evaluation Sheet (from Appendix 1) that your teacher returned to you to see specifically what you need to improve. Then consider the questions in the checklist below. Finally, rewrite your paper to make it clearer and more meaningful.

**CHECKLIST**

**Content**

Do you have a clear sentence that states what your composition is about?

Do all of your points connect directly to the topic?

Do you include enough details to make your point of view clear to your reader?

Is your composition interesting?

**Organization**

Do you have a clear set of main ideas in your composition?

Do all of your supporting details support your main ideas?

**Grammar**

Do you use gerunds and infinitives correctly?

**Reading 2: Extending the Topic Reading**

In this reading you will learn about how remittance dollars play an important and growing role in the economies of developing nations.

As you read this article, think about how the flow of remittance dollars affects the host nation *and* the recipient nation.

## The Remittance Lifeline[8]

### Funding by Individuals

1    A growing slice of the money that richer nations send to poorer nations does not come from investment by businesses or aid from governments. It comes instead from the cleaner who vacuums offices late in the evening. It comes from the undocumented[9] worker who picks the fruit we eat. It comes from the laborer who washes dishes as a second or third job at a late-night restaurant. Often, an important percentage of the earnings of these workers goes back to their home countries—sometimes to put food on their families' tables and sometimes to provide money for housing or a small business.

### Growing Numbers of Remittance Dollars

2    It is difficult to estimate how many remittance dollars move from one country to another each year. The reason is that much of the money moves by unofficial

[8] *lifeline:* a means by which life can exist
[9] *undocumented:* not having any legal papers

means, not through banks. However, some studies put the total for all countries for 2002 at $80 billion and, for 2003, at more than $140 billion. Furthermore, the World Bank's figures indicate that in some places—particularly South Asia—remittances are far greater than all other forms of funding. For instance, foreign direct investment (FDI) into South Asia was close to $5 billion in 2002. Remittances in the same year were more than $16 billion.

### Remittance Costs

3    It i         ificant that remittance money goes directly to people in need, not
th·                nts or foreign businesses. The only cost is getting the money
                   other. According to the World Bank, this cost can be as low
                        nittance amount for unofficial (and usually illegal) money
                        s 15 percent or more for licensed dealers.
                        er countries could help poorer countries is by
                        ittances. These fees, including all costs, can total
                        nt that is sent. Reducing these fees would
in                     greatly, benefiting the recipient countries.
The                    s of revenue is tiny for the richer host[10]
country,               recipient country. Such a change would
probably c             ice workers as well.

### People Export

5    Remittances see.                        .n for the poorer recipient
countries and the riche.                      .ntry gets the money it so badly
needs. The other country ge.          .J are prepared to do the jobs that many
non-immigrants are less willing t.

6    On the other hand, as the number of remittance workers increases, the export of people also increases. People who could be skilled workers in their home countries leave to become servants and cleaners. "Poor countries can't earn decent revenues by exporting coffee and cocoa, so they export people instead," says the director of the New Economics Foundation in London. These people, unfortunately, will no longer contribute to the stability of the economy in their home countries.

### More to Come?

7    For the near future, it seems clear that remittances will play an increasing part in the development of poorer countries. Remittance payments are rapidly increasing as richer countries continue to draw in immigrants. So the cleaner, the waiter, the farm laborer, and the building site worker will—unnoticed by most—continue to support their home countries on the path to development.

[10] *host:* a person who receives guests in his or her home or elsewhere

**Discussion** Discuss these questions with your classmates. You may wish to take notes to use when you write your composition in Activity 20.

1. Where does most of the money that poorer countries receive from richer countries come from?

2. What is this money used for?

3. Why is it difficult to know the total amount sent in remittances each year?

4. What are two reasons why remittances are good for the country that receives them?

5. Why are remittances good for the host country? Do you agree that this is good? Why or why not?

6. Why are remittances bad for the recipient country? What might be a better solution?

7. Considering the good and bad points of remittances, do you think that the whole process is more positive or more negative? Explain your answer. Give examples from the reading.

ACTIVITY 12 **Group Activity** In a group of 3–4 students, look at question 7 in Activity 11. Decide as a group whether "The Remittance Lifeline" overall is positive or negative. Try to agree within your group. Then decide what the biggest advantage is. Next decide what the biggest disadvantage is. Report your answers to the class.

**Circle one:** positive    negative

**Biggest advantage:** _____

_____

**Biggest disadvantage:** _____

_____

## Vocabulary

ACTIVITY 13 **Academic Words** Vocabulary words (in **boldface**) and their definitions are listed below. Choose the correct word from the list to complete sentences 1–10. Be sure to use the correct form of the word.

| | |
|---|---|
| **benefit** | to help |
| **economy** | the system of buying and selling that supports a country |
| **estimate** | to calculate the approximate worth, quantity, or size of something |
| **export** | the transport or selling of something to another country |

| **funding** | a sum of money set aside for a specific purpose |
| **licensed** | official or done with legal permission |
| **revenue** | income produced by a particular source |
| **significant** | having a major effect; important |
| **stability** | reliability or resistance to change |
| **transfer** | the movement of something from one place to another |

1. Sending a remittance requires a _____ agent if the sender does not have a bank account or a credit card.

2. The money a remittance worker sends home from the United States may

   be _____ enough to support five or six people in another country.

3. When one family member becomes a remittance worker, it _____ everyone else in the family.

4. A lack of money delayed the building project because the _____ came in slowly.

5. The most valuable resource that a poor country can _____ may be its people.

6. Currently, most _____ money-transfer firms cost the remittance sender much more than unofficial agents.

7. A high rate of employment is an important part of a country's economic

   _____.

8. It is hard to _____ how much remittance money it takes to support a large family.

9. A country needs to produce goods and services that people need in order to

   have an _____ that provides for its people.

10. Remittance transfers can be a good source of _____ for the firms who handle them.

# Composition Analysis

**Topic Sentences as Predictors** **Topic sentences** are one kind of main idea statement. They help readers predict the kind of information that the detail statements in the rest of the paragraph will include. Look at the following topic sentence:

> Because remittance costs are high, remittance workers have found many unofficial ways to send their money home.

Given this topic sentence, what will the details in the rest of the paragraph probably be about? A likely answer is: The rest of the paragraph will give details describing some unofficial ways that remittance workers have found to send their money home more cheaply.

**ACTIVITY 14** Read each of the following topic sentences. Because you do not have the context of the topic sentence or any details, you will not know for certain what the paragraph will be about. However, if you think carefully, you can make a good guess. Then circle the letter of the statement that best describes what the details in the rest of the paragraph will be about.

1. **Topic Sentence:** For several reasons, the most reliable money-transfer agents are banks and other large financial institutions.

   a. Reasons why banks in other countries sometimes go out of business

   b. Reasons why banks and other large financial institutions are growing

   c. Reasons why workers can trust banks and other large financial institutions to send their money

2. **Topic Sentence:** The remittance life can be hard when workers spend almost nothing on themselves so they can send more money home.

   a. Examples of workers who send nearly every penny that they earn home

   b. Reasons why families want to send remittance workers to the United States

   c. Reasons why spending little on themselves is a good idea for remittance workers

3. **Topic Sentence:** The cost of wiring money to their home countries is a significant expense that migrant workers face.

   a. The advantages and disadvantages of places that migrant workers can go to wire money

   b. Examples of how much it costs the sender to send remittances

   c. The requirements of setting up a bank account to send remittances

4. **Topic Sentence:** Many workers who send money home are frustrated by the difficulties of sending a remittance payment.

   a. How hard it is to successfully make remittance payments

   b. How much remittance payments are needed by many families

   c. How the reliability of unofficial remittance agents is causing some workers to reconsider sending remittance payments

5. **Topic Sentence:** Banks could improve their service to remittance workers in several ways.

   What will the details in the rest of the paragraph probably be about? (*You give an answer.*)

   _____

   _____

## Making Connections

You practiced locating details to support main ideas in the activities for Reading 1. Reading 2 also includes main ideas that can be supported by details in Reading 1. Finding these details will show the connections between Readings 1 and 2.

ACTIVITY 15    Look at the following main idea statements from Reading 2. Find supporting details from Reading 1 that support these main ideas. The first one is done for you.

1. **Main Idea from Reading 2:** ... an important percentage of [remittance workers'] earnings go back to their home countries—sometimes to put food on their families' tables and sometimes to provide money for housing or a small business.

   **Supporting Detail from Reading 1:** _Karen ... makes $460 a month working as a waitress and a babysitter. From that, she sends $300 home ..._

2. **Main Idea from Reading 2:** It is also significant that remittance money goes directly to people in need, not through governments or foreign businesses.

   **Supporting Detail from Reading 1:** _____

   _____

   _____

3. **Main Idea from Reading 2:** Remittances seem to be a win-win situation both for the poorer recipient countries and the richer host nations. One country gets the money it so badly needs. The other country gets workers who are prepared to do the jobs that many non-immigrants are less willing to do.

**Supporting Detail from Reading 1:** _____

_____

_____

4. **Main Idea from Reading 2:** "Poor countries can't earn decent revenues by exporting coffee and cocoa, so they export people instead," ... These people, unfortunately, will no longer contribute to the stability of the economy in their home countries.

**Supporting Detail from Reading 1:** _____

_____

_____

**ACTIVITY 16**   Reading 2 provides general information about the role of remittances in the economies of recipient and host countries. Think about the specific details you found in Activity 15 to support the main ideas in Reading 2. How would you describe the specific information in Reading 1?

**Kind of information in Reading 1:** _____

_____

## Reading 3: Academic Reading

### Sending Money Back Home

1    Money remittances are big business. Every year immigrants in North America and Europe send more than $60 billion to their home countries. Just over half of all global remittances come from the United States and sixty-five percent of that money goes to Latin America—the homeland of thirty-four million U.S. residents. Most of these funds are sent through small neighborhood businesses. Furthermore, estimates show that remitters collected about $12 billion in fees last year and this figure continues to grow. These facts suggest that banks and other major financial institutions should consider getting into the business of money transfers. After all, they are in a better position to serve the needs of customers than the mostly small businesses that now compete in this market. Banks can offer greater reliability, greater speed, and certainly lower fees.

2    Many immigrants are dissatisfied not only with the poor reliability and speed of the present informal remittance networks, but also with the huge fees they must pay. They may pay 6–15 percent of the remitted amount for the transaction. On top of that, they pay another 3–5 percent above the exchange rate for changing dollars to another currency.[11]

[11] *currency:* the kind of money used in a specific country

## Homeward Bound

Estimate of Remittances Sent from North America and Europe by Destination, 2001[1]

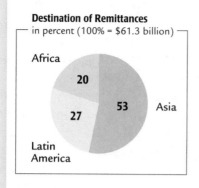

**Destination of Remittances**
in percent (100% = $61.3 billion)

Africa 20
Asia 53
Latin America 27

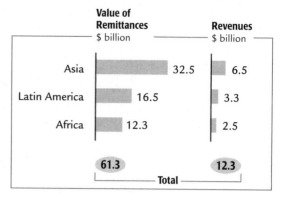

| | Value of Remittances $ billion | Revenues $ billion |
|---|---|---|
| Asia | 32.5 | 6.5 |
| Latin America | 16.5 | 3.3 |
| Africa | 12.3 | 2.5 |
| **Total** | **61.3** | **12.3** |

[1]Estimates based on distribution of 1993 data (most recent available on country-by-country basis); revenue estimates based on 1990–98 data and assume revenues = 20% of remittance value.
*Source:* World Bank; McKinsey analysis

### Chart 1

## A Valuable Market

Estimate of Remittances Sent from North America and Europe to Latin America by Country, 2001[1]

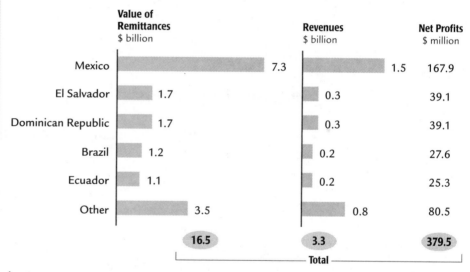

| | Value of Remittances $ billion | Revenues $ billion | Net Profits $ million |
|---|---|---|---|
| Mexico | 7.3 | 1.5 | 167.9 |
| El Salvador | 1.7 | 0.3 | 39.1 |
| Dominican Republic | 1.7 | 0.3 | 39.1 |
| Brazil | 1.2 | 0.2 | 27.6 |
| Ecuador | 1.1 | 0.2 | 25.3 |
| Other | 3.5 | 0.8 | 80.5 |
| **Total** | **16.5** | **3.3** | **379.5** |

[1]Estimates based on distribution of 1993 data (most recent available on country-by-country basis); assumes revenues = 20% of remittance value and net profit margin = 11.5% of revenues.
*Source:* World Bank; McKinsey analysis

### Chart 2

3  Currently, for those few immigrants who have bank accounts, transferring money through banks can be even more expensive. There are high minimum fees, and an enormous amount of paperwork is required even for small transfers. In the past, banks have shown little interest in serving the needs of immigrants. This is beginning to change, however, with the increasing numbers of immigrants using credit cards and checking accounts.

4  As a result, the market has new providers, including International Remittance Network (IRnet), which offers an electronic fund-transfer service. Members can

transfer money to local Citibank branches in El Salvador, Guatemala, and Mexico for $6.50 per transaction. This is one of the lowest fees in the market.

5    However, banks and other major financial institutions still have plenty of room to improve in how they deliver what customers want: reliability, speed, reasonable prices, and more products. Because immigrants need to send money home for much more than groceries, they must have new services. They need efficient ways to send money for land purchases, mortgages, utility bills, personal investments, and even new homes. Banks are in a good position to develop creative new products with their own branch networks for mortgage payments, with utilities for electric, gas, and water bills, and with real-estate companies for land and house payments. One new product already available is a system for automatic debits[12] from a wire transfer.[13]

6    To enter the money remittance market, banks should consider building connections with local partners. Those with such networks in recipient countries could easily benefit from the remittance opportunity. Wells Fargo and Citibank, for example, now accept the *matricula consular* (an identity card issued by Mexican consulates) as identification for immigrants who wish to open accounts.

7    In all these ways, money remittance services for immigrants clearly represent a profitable[14] opportunity for financial institutions ready to offer them a better deal.

[12] *debits:* payments that come directly from a bank account
[13] *wire transfer:* an electronic movement of funds
[14] *profitable:* money making

## Composition Analysis

**A Cause and Effect Essay**   A **cause and effect** essay focuses on a situation, action, or event that leads to a result or effect. In Reading 3, the main **cause** is the need for more efficient, less expensive ways for immigrants to send remittances. The **effect** is the opportunity that large financial institutions have to fill this need.

Sometimes one cause may have more than one effect. The main point in Reading 3 is that banks could benefit from acting as remittance agents. However, some of the same information could also be used to support the point of view that immigrants would benefit. Look at the following example.

> ... banks and other major financial institutions should consider getting into the business of money transfers. After all, they are in a better position to serve the needs of customers than the mostly small businesses that now compete in this market.

**Effect 1:** Serving the remittance needs of customers would be profitable for banks and other major financial institutions.

**Effect 2:** Using banks and other major financial institutions to send remittances would better serve the needs of customers than using small businesses.

Look at the following sentences from Reading 3. Write an effect for each one. Each effect should support the point of view that immigrants would benefit if banks got into the remittance business. (Your answers do not have to be complete sentences.) The first one is done for you.

1. ... banks and other major financial institutions should consider getting into [the business of money transfers.] After all, they are in a better position to serve the needs of customers than the mostly small businesses that now compete in this market.

   **Effect on immigrants:** _would serve their remittance needs better than_

   _small businesses_

2. ... banks and other major financial institutions still have plenty of room to improve in how they deliver what customers want: reliability, speed, reasonable prices, and more products.

   **Effect on immigrants:** _____

   _____

3. Banks are in a good position to develop creative new products with their own branch networks for mortgage payments, with utilities for electric, gas, and water bills, and with real-estate companies for land and house payments.

   **Effect on immigrants:** _____

   _____

4. ... money remittance services for immigrants clearly represent a profitable opportunity for financial institutions ready to offer them a better deal.

   **Effect on immigrants:** _____

   _____

**Using Charts to Show Support in an Essay** Charts are a good way to provide information that is useful in supporting the main ideas in an essay. Look again at paragraph 1 of Reading 3, "Sending Money Back Home."

The point of view in this paragraph is that large banks and other financial institutions would make money if they got more involved in the remittance process. If they did, they would also do a service to existing customers. Chart 1 supports this point in at least two ways. First, it shows that most remittances go to continents, such as Asia and Latin America, from which large populations have moved to the United States. Second, it shows the enormous value of remittance payment revenues. Both ideas help the reader to conclude that even at lower customer rates, there is still good profit for banks that act as remittance agents.

**Find supporting details for the following statements about Charts 1 and 2. The first one is done for you.**

1. More remittance revenues come from money sent to Asia than all other destinations combined.

    **Detail from chart:** *$6.5 billion out of a total of $12.3 billion in remittance revenues come from Asia.*

2. Even at 10 percent of remittance value, the total revenues from all remittances would be enormous.

    **Detail from chart:** _____

    _____

3. The net profits from remittances to Mexico equals more than one third of the net profits from remittances to all of Latin America.

    **Detail from chart:** _____

    _____

4. If total net profits were only 10 percent of remittance value instead of 11.5 percent, profits would still be huge.

    **Detail from chart:** _____

    _____

5. Offering remittance services could mean big business for banks and other large financial institutions.

    **Detail from chart:** _____

    _____

# *Writing 2*

**ACTIVITY 19**

To help you prepare for the writing assignment in the next section, choose a topic and discuss the questions with a partner who has chosen the same topic as you. Write answers to the questions in your own words. You do not need to agree with your partner as long as you can give reasons for your answers.

### Topic 1

1. What are at least two reasons that banks are better remittance agents than informal neighborhood businesses?

2. Can you support your answers with information from the readings and charts?

### Topic 2

1. Based on the readings in this chapter, what do you think are the most positive aspects of remittances?

2. Can you give reasons from the readings or your personal experience that support your answers?

### Topic 3

1. Based on the readings in this chapter, what do you think are the most negative aspects of remittances?

2. Can you give reasons from the readings or your personal experience that support your answers?

**ACTIVITY 20**

Write a cause and effect composition about one of the following topics. You may wish to look back at the work you did in Activity 17 and the notes you took in Activity 11.

### Topic 1

Write about three reasons why immigrants benefit if banks act as their remittance agents. Use information from Reading 2 or Reading 3 (including the charts) to support your answer.

### Topic 2

Consider what you have learned in this chapter about remittances and how they work. Write a composition about *the three most positive effects* of them. Give reasons from the readings in this chapter to support your opinion and be sure to include any personal experiences or knowledge you may have.

### Topic 3

Consider what you have learned in this chapter about remittances and how they work. Write a composition about *the three most negative effects* of them. Give reasons from the readings in this chapter to support your opinion and be sure to include any personal experiences or knowledge you may have.

## Modal Auxiliaries

**Modal auxiliaries** are verbs. They appear before the main verb in a clause or sentence. Modal verbs change or modify the meaning of verbs. For example, modals can express necessity, possibility, past possibility, advisability, etc. Often modals have more than one meaning. Look at the following examples from Reading 2 and Reading 3. The modals are boldface.

1 Because immigrants send money home for much more than groceries, they **must** have new services.

In this sentence, the modal *must* expresses necessity. The meaning of the verb also changes: "they *must* have" means they do not yet have, but "they have" means they do have.

2 They **may** pay 6–15 percent of the remitted amount for the transaction.

In this sentence, the modal *may* expresses possibility (but not strong possibility). The meaning of the verb also changes: "they *may* pay" means they might pay, but "they pay" means they do pay.

3 These fees, including all costs, **can** total as much as 20 percent of the amount that is sent.

In this sentence, the modal *can* expresses strong possibility. The meaning of the verb also changes: "fees *can* total" means fees possibly total, but "fees total" means they do total.

4 An important way that richer countries **could** help poorer countries is by reducing the cost of sending remittances.

In this sentence, the modal *could* expresses past strong possibility. The meaning of the verb also changes: "countries *could* help" means countries currently do not help, but "countries help" means countries do help.

5 These facts suggest that banks and other major financial institutions **should** consider getting into the business of money transfers.

In this sentence, the modal *should* expresses advisability. The meaning of the verb also changes: "institutions *should* consider" means institutions do not consider, but "institutions consider" means institutions do consider.

Modals have only one form. No final *-s* is added for the third person singular, and modals do not change based on verb tense. Modals are immediately followed by the base form of a verb.

Circle the letter of the statement that best describes the meaning of each numbered sentence.

1. I could have taken a vacation before I started applying for jobs.

   a. I took a vacation.

   b. I had the opportunity to take a vacation.

   c. I was thinking of taking a vacation.

2. You should join a study group if you want to improve your grades.

   a. It will probably improve your grades to join a study group.

   b. It is necessary that you join a study group.

   c. It might improve your grades to join a study group.

3. Remittance workers must spend long periods of time away from their families.

   a. Remittance workers probably spend long periods of time away from their families.

   b. Remittance workers possibly spend long periods of time away from their families.

   c. Remittance workers definitely spend long periods of time away from their families.

4. Receiving remittance dollars can make a big difference to low income families.

   a. Remittance dollars are making a big difference to low income families.

   b. Remittance dollars often make a big difference to low income families.

   c. Remittance dollars always make a big difference to low income families.

5. When I visit my family in Mexico, I may stay for a month.

   a. I will stay for a month.

   b. I will possibly stay for a month.

   c. I will probably not stay for a month, but I might.

Correct the six modal and verb form errors in the paragraph below using modals from the list below.

| may | can | could | should | must |
|-----|-----|-------|--------|------|

Jesus came to the United States one year ago. He thought he can earn more money and sends it to his family in Nicaragua. His father is suffering from diabetes and has missed many weeks of work. In addition, he has a lot of medical bills. Jesus thinks his father should cut down on his work. He also thinks if he may send enough money, his father may will decide to work less. Jesus wishes he must be with his father and the rest of his family, but he knows he must worked hard to earn as much money as he can as a remittance worker. This is the most important thing that can make a difference to his family.

## Rewriting 2

ACTIVITY 23 **Peer Activity** Trade your composition from Activity 20 with another student. Read your partner's paper and underline the topic sentence. Then do one of the following:

1. If your partner wrote about Topic 1, make a list of the three important reasons why immigrants benefit if banks act as their agents for sending remittances. You do not need to write complete sentences. Then check to see if the composition has supporting details for each of these reasons.

2. If your partner wrote about Topic 2, make a list of the three most positive aspects of remittances. You do not need to write complete sentences. Then check to see if the composition has supporting details for each of these aspects.

3. If your partner wrote about Topic 3, make a list of the three most negative aspects of remittances. You do not need to write complete sentences. Then check to see if the composition has supporting details for each of these aspects.

Next, talk to your partner about what you found and help him or her make any necessary changes.

**ACTIVITY 24**    **On Your Own** Review your partner's notes, your partner's comments, and your teacher's feedback on the first draft of your composition. Use the Composition Evaluation Sheet (from Appendix 1) that your teacher returned to you to see specifically what you need to improve. Then consider the questions in the checklist below. Finally, rewrite your paper to make it clearer and more meaningful.

**✔CHECKLIST**

**Content**

Do you have a clear topic sentence that states the purpose of your composition?

Do you clearly state the effects of your three specific reasons?

**Organization**

Do the details and examples support your topic sentence(s)?

Do you have any sentences that do not connect to your topic?

**Grammar**

Do you use gerunds and infinitives correctly?

Do you use modals correctly?

## Internet Activities

For additional activities related to this chapter, go to elt.thomson.com/catalyst.

# CHAPTER 2

# Discrimination

## Exploring the Topic

**ACTIVITY 1**

**Discussion** People feel comfortable with people who are similar to themselves. However, in a diverse country like the United States, people of many different nationalities live, work, and sit next to each other every day. Much of the time this causes no problem, but ideas about a group of people who seem different may cause people to become uncomfortable. Such stereotypes are always based on lack of knowledge and are always too general; however, they may be widely accepted.

In groups of 3–4, discuss the following ideas and questions. Then share your ideas with the class.

1. Think of a person that you did not like at first, but later when you got to know the person, your feelings changed. Talk about your experience.

2. What stereotypes are common among people you know or live with? Where do you think these stereotypes came from?

3. Has your idea about a group of people changed since you learned more about them? Tell about your experience.

29

## Reading 1: Personal Experience Reading

Here are three stories about immigrants who suffered the negative effects of discrimination but were able to turn their experiences around to create something positive. These are strong and imaginative people who use their abilities to make a bad situation better.

Pay attention to the methods that these immigrants use to improve the discriminatory situations in their lives. You will use your thoughts later in this chapter.

## A Land of Diversity[1]

1   America has been a land of immigrants from the beginning. The first immigrants were white people from England and other western European countries. Soon the Europeans were bringing black slaves[2] by force from West Africa to help develop their agriculture. Over time, many other immigrants arrived who also looked very different from the original Europeans. Between 1820 and 1930, over thirty million European immigrants came to the United States, over a million Asians arrived from Japan and China, and over four million immigrants came from Latin America. Those who looked white had less trouble; those who looked darker, especially the black African slaves, had more trouble. Americans continued to feel most comfortable with people who looked more like themselves.

2   Since the 1970s, the world has become more socially and economically integrated.[3] New waves of immigrants are arriving in the United States. Over seven million new Asian and over ten million new Latin American immigrants have

[1] *diversity:* variety, differences
[2] *slave:* a person owned by another person for the purpose of doing hard work
[3] *integrated:* joined, united

settled in the United States in the last thirty years. Most are non-whites; that is, they don't look very European or "American." Consequently, it has often been difficult for new immigrants to fit in with Americans at school, at work, and at play. Let's consider three of their stories.

## Story One

3    My name is Keema and I am seventeen years old. I have lived in Chicago for two years now. I came from Kenya, in East Africa. I always believed that America was a great country, and that I would be accepted and have a good time. I didn't realize how wrong I was. This is a great country, for sure, but when I started school, I got some bad reactions. Kids said things like, "You 'dumba' of an African, why don't you go back where you came from?" I was shocked, but I thought, they don't know anything about me. I felt it was wrong and I decided I wouldn't let anyone treat me that way.

4    I realized most of the kids at my school were ignorant. But that isn't an excuse for treating others badly. I believe no child is born a racist. They learn it. So a few friends and I have started a Diversity Club at school with the help of one Puerto Rican teacher and one black teacher from the South Side. We have started a newsletter, put up posters, given some talks in classes, and held an evening talent show. The kids at school almost never call me names anymore.

5    Many times when I walk down the street, I know people don't realize I am a new immigrant from Africa. They think I am an American black. I know that many people think they are inferior so I feel they look down on me too. I am hopeful that as more of us come from Africa and other places, Americans will accept us more openly and without prejudice due to our appearance or the color of our skin.

## Story Two

6    My name is Park Kyo-Gun. I am from the small country of Korea. Many Koreans have immigrated to the United States, especially California, in the past sixty years. I came too after our last war ended and have lived here for forty years. I live quietly with my family and own a small grocery business on a busy street in Los Angeles.

7    My family had trouble in this city for a long time. My children often didn't have many friends at school. Our neighbors rarely talked to us. When people came to the store, they did not try to communicate with us. They spoke to my wife and me in loud voices. They skipped words in their sentences. They treated us this way when they heard our accents, even though I speak English well enough. My store was robbed twice. I knew that my black neighbors also had troubles, but we never talked about it together.

8    A few years ago, the whole East Side of Los Angeles erupted into a riot. Many of our neighbors, the blacks and the Mexicans, were so angry at the society around them that they hurt everyone; they burned, destroyed, and looted thousands of businesses and homes. We didn't really understand the reasons, but we were in the middle of it. We just watched the city burn.

9    Afterwards, I decided to make some changes. I began to put some Korean decorations around our store, and I smiled and greeted everyone who came in. I also put up a list of Mexican and other holidays. I found a neighborhood association and attended some meetings to learn more about the different ethnic[4]

---

[4] *ethnic:* relating to the same cultural group

groups in our area. Also, my own children began to tell me more about life outside our family and Korean culture. I listened and learned, and today I feel better about my neighborhood. I know my customers feel more comfortable in my store too.

### Story Three

10    My name is Anu Baghosian and my parents came from Iran twenty-five years ago. I was born in Boston and went to the University of Massachusetts. Of course, I speak English without any accent, though my parents still have strong accents. I am happy with my life here in America, and I understand how lucky my parents were to escape from Iran when they did. Yet when I tell people my family came from Iran, I often get a strange reaction. They look at me like I'm an Arab terrorist[5] or something.

11    First I have to tell them that Iran is not an Arab country, and I don't even speak Arabic. Persian is related to Sanskrit, an ancient language of India. Then I tell them that I am not Muslim, though I can't understand why they think every Muslim must be a bad person. We come from a long history of Christians in Persia. Finally I tell them I am American, born and raised here. But they don't understand. They look at me, listen to my name, and then raise their eyebrows. I know what that means now.

12    Last year at the university, I met a new boy. He has dark skin and dark eyes like me. His family is Greek though they have lived in the United States for several generations. We went out for a few months and I began to like him a lot. Finally I got to meet his parents. They looked at me funny at first, and then they asked about my religion. When I told them I am Christian, they smiled and shook my hand, but they still didn't understand how a Christian could come from Iran. I showed them some pictures of our family back home. They were happy to learn about my family and our history. I hope Basil and I can marry next year.

### Communication Is the Key

13    These stories are about different people and different struggles. Yet in one sense they are all the same. The speakers all experienced a form of misunderstanding in America—discrimination. One way they coped, as we have seen, was to step forward and communicate in some way with classmates, customers, neighbors, and acquaintances. They learned about other immigrants, shared information about themselves, and participated in the diverse culture of the United States. These actions presented the opportunity for meaningful understanding as well as for discovering similarities.

5 *terrorist:* someone who uses violence to attack societies or governments

ACTIVITY 2      **Discussion** Discuss these questions with your classmates. You may wish to take some notes to use later in your writing assignment.

1. Do you feel more comfortable with people who look more like yourself? Give an example.

2. Why do you think the white Europeans made slaves of black Africans instead of another group of people?

3. Why do you think people form stereotypes?

4. Choose a group of people and write as many stereotypes as you have heard about these people. Discuss where you think these stereotypes came from. Do you think any of them are true?

5. What makes people give up their stereotypes? Give an example.

6. Explain one possible reason why you think the person in each story in Reading 1 experienced discrimination.

**ACTIVITY 3**

Personal stories in writing often show readers essential truths about human life, such as "Necessity is the mother of invention." In Reading 1, Keema, Park Kyo-Gun, and Anu Baghosian use personal experiences to show how they encountered discrimination and what they did about it.

Think about what each of these people did in response to the discrimination they felt. Then think about how their reactions are similar. What is one factor that each of their solutions has in common?

_____

_____

_____

## Vocabulary

**ACTIVITY 4**

**Academic Words** Write the letter of the correct definition in front of each new word.

| Words | Meanings |
|---|---|
| _____ 1. **diverse** | a. a person who believes that one race is better than others |
| _____ 2. **participate** | b. to break out or begin suddenly |
| _____ 3. **riot** | c. to relieve stress or tension |
| _____ 4. **ignorant** | d. an outbreak of violence |
| _____ 5. **relax** | e. unaware |
| _____ 6. **racist** | f. a response to something |
| _____ 7. **erupt** | g. all of the people living at the same time or of a certain age |
| _____ 8. **reaction** | h. to take part in something |
| _____ 9. **generation** | i. including different kinds or forms of things |
| _____ 10. **similarity** | j. quality of being like or equivalent |

# Composition Analysis

**Controlling Ideas**  In Chapter 1, you learned that topic sentences tell the kind of information you will find in the rest of the paragraph. A topic sentence can also contain the writer's point of view in a controlling idea. The **controlling idea** tells the writer's opinion about the topic so that the topic sentence is not just a statement of fact. It also narrows the topic and presents the focus of the paragraph. It is the part of the topic sentence that readers can ask questions about and that they expect to find answered in the detail sentences of the paragraph. Look at the following topic sentences. The controlling ideas are in boldface.

A During difficult economic times immigrants often become **the victims of racism and hatred**.

This *is* an effective topic sentence because the reader wonders how and why immigrants become the victims of racism and hatred.

B Non-white immigrants are treated **more unfairly** than white immigrants for two reasons.

This *is* an effective topic sentence because the reader expects to read about two reasons why non-white immigrants are treated more unfairly.

C Immigrants create **understanding and acceptance** when they communicate with other people in several simple ways.

This *is* an effective topic sentence because it lets the reader know that the paragraph will be about ways that immigrants can communicate with other people to create understanding and acceptance.

D Immigrants experience discrimination.

This *is not* an effective topic sentence because it does not have a controlling idea to communicate the writer's point of view. We do not know how the writer will develop this information in the paragraph. The sentence is also very general.

E Hate crimes are one form of discrimination.

This *is not* an effective topic sentence because it is a simple fact. There is no controlling idea and no point of view. It does not introduce an idea that the reader can ask questions about. There is no more to say.

---

**ACTIVITY 5**  Circle the letter of the sentence in each pair that is the best topic sentence. Then write a question that you would expect a paragraph with this topic sentence to answer. The first one is done for you.

1. (a.) Discrimination hurts everyone, not just people who are discriminated against.

   b. Discrimination is the unfair treatment of a person based on race.

   **Question:** _How does discrimination hurt everyone?_

2. a. Discrimination occurs between people who are different.

   b. Discrimination is difficult for immigrants to deal with for three reasons.

   **Question:** _____

   _____

3. a. Stereotypes are general ideas about a certain group of people.

   b. Stereotypes are harmful because they lead to discrimination.

   **Question:** _____

   _____

4. a. The desire for freedom and opportunity is what drives immigrants to work so hard.

   b. Immigrants always work hard.

   **Question:** _____

   _____

5. a. Between 1820 and 1930, over thirty million European immigrants came to the United States.

   b. The United States was the land of opportunity for thirty million European immigrants between 1820 and 1930.

   **Question:** _____

   _____

6. a. Communication between races is the path to understanding differences.

   b. Sometimes communication exists between races.

   **Question:** _____

   _____

Write a topic sentence of your own for the following paragraph.

7. _____

   _____

During times of high unemployment, non-immigrant Americans fear that immigrants will fill too many jobs. Also, if immigrants have low-paying jobs, they contribute less in taxes, which pay for public services. If they have low-paying jobs, they will also put less money into the economy for food, clothing, housing, and other goods. Finally immigrants, who often are negatively stereotyped, are people non-immigrants can blame their troubles on during difficult economic times. These are all reasons why immigrants experience more acts of discrimination when times are hard.

# Writing 1

**ACTIVITY 6**

To help you prepare for the writing assignment in the next section, choose a topic and discuss the questions with a partner who has chosen the same topic as you. Write answers to the questions in your own words. You do not need to agree with your partner as long as you can give reasons for your answers.

### Topic 1

1. What misunderstanding did one of the characters in Reading 1 experience?

2. How did he or she try to improve understanding?

3. How have you tried to deal with acts of discrimination in your life?

### Topic 2

1. Describe a negative misunderstanding you once had about someone. Tell about what you first thought. Then tell about how your attitude improved.

2. Did you make any conclusions from your misunderstanding? If so, tell about them.

**ACTIVITY 7**

**Writing Assignment** Write a composition about one of the following topics. Be sure to include in your paper all of the items in the checklist on page 38. You may wish to use some of the notes you took in Activity 2 to give you ideas.

### Topic 1

Choose one of the stories in Reading 1 and describe the misunderstanding that the writer felt and how he or she tried to create understanding. Include a similar personal experience that you have had, and tell how you tried to cope with the situation.

### Topic 2

Tell about a time when your attitude about someone improved based on new information. Be sure to state your original negative attitude clearly in your topic sentence. Then tell how your attitude grew more positive.

# Grammar

<table>
<tr>
<td valign="top">

**Simple Past and Present Perfect Verb Tenses**

</td>
<td valign="top">

Look at the following sentences from the readings. Notice the verb tenses in **boldface**.

1 In America, the Gold Rush, agricultural and industrial development, and the construction of the transcontinental railway **offered** many possibilities for employment.
2 One of the many acts of discrimination **was** the detention of Chinese immigrants at Angel Island in the San Francisco Bay from 1910–1940.

Sentences 1 and 2 are about things that happened and were completed in the past. We use the **simple past tense** for this. We write the simple past tense by using the past tense form of the verb.

3 America **has been** a land of immigrants from the beginning.
4 Over seven million new Asian and over ten million new Latin American immigrants **have settled** in the United States in the last thirty years.

Sentences 3 and 4 are about things that started in the past, but continue up to the present. We use the **present perfect tense** for this. We write the present perfect tense by using the present tense form of the helping verb *to have* plus the past participle form of the main verb.

</td>
</tr>
</table>

**ACTIVITY 8**  Fill in the correct form of the verb in the following sentences. Use the simple past tense or the present perfect tense. To help you decide which tense to use, think about whether the action in the sentence is finished or not.

1. The first Europeans who came to America (**use**) _____ a system of slavery to help develop their agriculture.

2. America (**become**) _____ a land of diversity because of the many

   immigrants who (**settle**) _____ there in the last fifty years.

3. The detainees at Angel Island (**come**) _____ from China.

4. Much (**change**) _____ in America since the days of the Chinese Exclusion Act, but discrimination still exists.

5. After the Japanese (**attack**) _____ Pearl Harbor in 1941, 92,785 Californians of Japanese ancestry were sent to twenty-six internment camps over a four-year period.

6. Now that I (**travel**) _____ out of my own country, I understand better how immigrants feel when they come to the United States.

**ACTIVITY 9** Now write four sentences about yourself using the correct verb tense. Include the information given for each sentence.

1. the length of time of your stay in the United States

   I _____ in the United States for _____.

2. the date of your arrival in the United States

   I _____ in the United States on _____.

3. what you most liked about the United States on the day of your arrival

   On the day of my arrival, I _____ _____ the most.

4. something about Americans you still find difficult to deal with

   I _____

   _____ ever since I came to the United States.

## Rewriting 1

**ACTIVITY 10** **Peer Activity** Trade your paper from Activity 7 with another student. Read your partner's paper and underline the topic sentence in each paragraph. If you can't find a topic sentence, see if you can help your partner write one. Next, circle the controlling idea. Then tell your partner what you think is most interesting about his or her paper.

**ACTIVITY 11** **On Your Own** Review your partner's notes, your partner's comments, and your teacher's feedback on the first draft of your composition. Use the Composition Evaluation Sheet (from Appendix 1) that your teacher returned to you to see specifically what you need to improve. Then review your answers to the questions in the checklist below. Rewrite your paper to make it clearer and more meaningful.

---

**✓CHECKLIST**

**Content**
Do you attempt to persuade the reader of your point of view?
Do you include enough details to clearly explain your main idea?
Do you make interesting points?

**Organization**
Do you have a topic sentence that gives your point of view, narrows the topic, and predicts what information you will include?
Do you include only sentences that are related to your topic sentence?
Do your points follow a logical order?
Do you have a conclusion?

**Grammar**
Do you use the simple past and present perfect tenses correctly?

---

## Reading 2: Extending the Topic Reading

Some of the worst acts of discrimination in American history occurred against the Chinese. These included the Chinese Exclusion Act passed in 1882 and the detainment of Chinese immigrants at Angel Island from 1910–1940. These events were particularly hurtful because they took place just after a period when the Chinese were highly valued for their hard work in the development of a growing nation. Here are the personal accounts of three Angel Island detainees.

**Think about what made attitudes toward the Chinese change. There may be reasons you can think of that are not mentioned in the reading. You will use your thoughts later in this chapter.**

## A Historical Account of Discrimination Against the Chinese

1   The first large numbers of Chinese began arriving in the United States in the mid-1850s. Reasons for this immigration included over-population, years of drought,[6] floods, disease, and famine.[7] Political and economic difficulty in China also contributed. In America, on the other hand, the Gold Rush,[8] agricultural and industrial development, and the construction of the transcontinental[9] railway offered many possibilities for employment.

2   By the early 1870s, however, when the Gold Rush had ended, the U.S. economy was slowing down. A strong competition for jobs emerged. Unfortunately, the

[6] *drought:* a long period of low rainfall
[7] *famine:* food shortage
[8] *Gold Rush:* rush of people to an area of California where gold was discovered
[9] *transcontinental:* going across a continent

Chinese, who had once been valued for their tireless work, became the victims of racism and hatred. Laws were passed attacking their livelihoods and civil rights[10] and violence broke out against Chinese immigrants.

3    The Chinese Exclusion Act was passed in 1882. It denied all Chinese immigrants U.S. citizenship and suspended the immigration of Chinese for ten years. It was extended for additional ten-year periods in 1892 and again in 1902. In 1904, it was amended to be continuous. For the first time in American history, immigration into the United States was refused on the basis of nationality.

4    One of the many acts of discrimination during this time was the detention of Chinese immigrants at Angel Island in the San Francisco Bay from 1910–1940. Many immigration records were destroyed in the 1906 San Francisco earthquake and fire, so Chinese immigrants were held and interrogated at this immigration station. The purpose was to force them to prove that they had a relative who was a U.S. citizen. If they could not, they would be deported. U.S. officials hoped to deport as many as possible. They asked difficult, detailed questions about Chinese villages and family histories that immigrants would have trouble answering correctly. Immigrants were detained for weeks, months, sometimes even years. Here are three of their stories.

### Mrs. Chan, age 23 in 1939

5    When we first arrived, we were told to put down our luggage and they pushed us toward the buildings. More than 100 of us arrived. The men had their dormitories[11] and the women, theirs. They assigned us beds and there were white women to take care of us.

6    When we returned from the dining hall they locked the doors behind us. Once you were locked in, they didn't bother with you. It was like being in prison. Some read newspapers or books; some knitted.

7    There was a small fenced-in area for exercising, sunning, and ball playing. There were windows and we could see the boats arrive daily at about 9:30 or 10 AM. Once a week, they allowed us to walk out to the storage shed where our luggage was kept.

8    We could write as many letters as we wanted, but they examined our letters before mailing them. It was the same for letters coming in.

9    There were good friends, but there were also those who didn't get along. There were arguments, and people cried when they saw others who were fortunate enough to leave, especially those of us who had been there a long time. I must have cried a bowlful during my stay at Angel Island. I was there the longest and always the one left behind.

### Mr. Lowe, age 16 in 1939

10    I had nothing to do there. During the day, we stared at the scenery beyond the barbed wires[12]—the sea and the sky and the clouds that were separated from us. Besides listening to the birds outside the fence, we could listen to records and talk to old-timers in the barracks. Some, due to faulty responses during the interrogation and lengthy appeal procedures, had been there for years. They poured out their sorrow unceasingly.

10 *civil rights:* equal protection of individuals by law
11 *dormitory:* a building or sleeping area for many people
12 *barbed wires:* wires with sharp metal points

11    Their greatest misery stemmed from the fact that most of them had had to borrow money for their trips to America. Some sold their houses; some sold their land; some had to borrow at such high interest rates that their families had to sacrifice. A few committed suicide[13] in the detention barracks.

12    The worst part was the toilet. It was a ditch congested with filth.[14] It stank up the whole barracks. We slept on canvas bunks. The blankets were so coarse that they might have been woven of wolf's hair. It was indeed a most humiliating[15] imprisonment.

*Mr. Leung, age 24 in 1936*

13    When it was my turn to be interrogated, they first made me wait in a small room. After a while they called me in and started asking me this and that, this and that, until I had a headache. After three or four hours of this, they confined me to a downstairs room where I stayed overnight. The next day, they questioned me again. They very seldom questioned you one day only and allowed you to return upstairs.

14    One strange question they asked me was, "What is your living room floor made of?" I replied, "Brick." They said, "Okay. What is the floor under your bed made of?" So I thought if the living room floor was brick, then the bedroom floor must also be brick. So I said, "Brick!" The next day, they asked the same question and I replied, "Brick," again. They said my father had said it was dirt. What happened was that the floor was dirt at first, but later, after my father left for America, I changed the floor myself to brick.

15    Where I really went wrong was in answering the question about who gave me the money to come to America. My father had written that he would send the money home to my mother to give me so that's what I said. But what happened was my father didn't really have the money and another relative loaned the money to my mother. So although I was a real son, I failed the interrogation.

16    My deepest impression of Angel Island was the rudeness of the white interrogators. They kept saying, "Come on, answer, answer." They kept rushing me to answer until I couldn't remember the answers anymore. And it wasn't just the whites. The Chinese interpreters did it too.

---

[13] *committed suicide:* killed themselves
[14] *filth:* a very dirty bad-smelling substance
[15] *humiliating:* lowering self-respect

**ACTIVITY 12**    **Discussion** Discuss these questions with your classmates. You may wish to make some notes to use in the writing assignment in Activity 20.

1. Are any of the reasons for the Chinese immigration around 1850 similar to the reasons why people immigrate from your birth country? If so, what reasons? If not, what are other reasons why people immigrate?

2. Why do you think the Chinese were welcome at that time?

3. What happened that made attitudes toward the Chinese change? Do you think there were any other reasons for this change in attitude? Give an example.

4. What effect did this change in attitude have on the lives of the Chinese?

5. What methods did the detainees use to take their attention away from their situation?

6. What do you find interesting or surprising about detention life? Explain your answer.

7. What do you think of the way the U.S. officials treated the Chinese? Give examples to support your answer.

8. Why do you think this form of discrimination was accepted at the time?

ACTIVITY 13 **Group Activity** Imagine that you are a detainee at Angel Island. Write a letter to a family member in China describing your experience there and how you feel about it. When you have finished, form a group of 3–4 students. Read your letters to each other and discuss them. Your teacher may ask you to choose one letter to share with the class.

Dear _____,

It seems like a very long time since we sat together face to face. Each morning I feel _____ as I begin the long wait for the freedom I came here for. Then in the afternoon there are the endless questions that make me feel _____

_____

_____.

To pass the time I _____

_____.

I have seen things here that I never imagined I would see in America, for example, _____

_____.

At night when I lie in my bed, I think about _____

_____

_____.

The most important thing I want to tell you is _____

_____.

With love,

_____

# Vocabulary

ACTIVITY 14 **Academic Words** Fill in each blank with the correct word from the list of Academic Word List words below. Be sure to use the correct word form.

| Words | Meanings |
|---|---|
| **amended** | changed |
| **confined** | to be restricted or kept in |
| **construction** | the building of something |
| **denied** | refused |
| **deported** | forced to leave a country |
| **emerged** | came out |
| **interrogated** | intensively questioned |
| **livelihood** | the way a person makes a living |
| **procedure** | a manner of doing something |
| **suspended** | stopped for a time; interrupted |

1. The _____ of the new school took much longer than expected.

2. When the final witness told his story, the truth _____.

3. The _____ that the U.S. officials used to interrogate the Chinese was disrespectful and rude.

4. Many Chinese were _____ because they could not answer some of the very difficult, detailed questions the inspectors asked.

5. Classes were _____ for the day because of the snowstorm.

6. Our plan was _____ to include one less person when one of our members got sick.

7. Immigrants must often take up a new _____ to earn a living in a new country.

8. His application for a visa was _____ so he had to give up his travels.

9. Often the detainees were _____ for many hours at a time for questioning.

10. To _____ someone is not always the best way to get the answers you are looking for.

**ACTIVITY 15** Many words have more than one form. For example the verb *accomplish* also has a noun form, *accomplishment*, and an adjective form, *accomplished*. If you understand how word forms are made, you can greatly increase your vocabulary.

Fill in the missing word forms in the chart below. Use your dictionary to check word forms you don't know. An X means that there is no common word form for a certain part of speech. (See Appendix 5, Word Form Suffixes, on page 219.)

| Noun (Thing) | Verb | Adjective | Adverb |
|---|---|---|---|
| construction | | | X |
| | | emerging | X |
| | | | deniably |
| | suspend | | X |
| amendment | | | X |
| | | | procedurally |
| | confine | | X |
| deportation | | | X |
| | interrogate | | X |

## Composition Analysis

**Narration** When giving historical information, writers will sometimes use narrative accounts, or a description of events, by people who were present, to support their facts. For example:

**Historical Fact**

> Unfortunately, the Chinese who had once been valued for their tireless work became the victims of racism and hatred.

**Narrative Account from Mrs. Chan**

> When we returned from the dining hall they locked the doors behind us. Once you were locked in, they didn't bother with you. It was like being in prison.

Find a narrative account in Reading 2 that supports each of the following historical facts. Give the name of the speaker and write what he or she said.

1. One of the many acts of discrimination during [the time when the Chinese Exclusion Act was in effect], was the detention of Chinese immigrants at Angel Island in the San Francisco Bay from 1910–1940.

   **Narrative Account from** _____:

   _____

   _____

2. U.S. officials hoped to deport as many [Chinese] as possible. They asked difficult, detailed questions about Chinese villages and family histories that immigrants would have trouble answering correctly.

   **Narrative Account from** _____:

   _____

   _____

3. Immigrants were detained for weeks, months, sometimes even years.

   **Narrative Account from** _____:

   _____

   _____

List another sentence from Reading 2 and a narrative account that supports it.

4. _____

   _____

   **Narrative Account from** _____:

   _____

   _____

# Making Connections

ACTIVITY 17 The following sentences describe feelings that two or more of the immigrants in Readings 1 and 2 experienced. For each sentence, give two or three examples from the narratives (stories) in the readings. The first one is done for you.

1. Other people think I am something I know I am not.

   a. _Classmates thought Keema was dumb._

   b. _Anu Baghosian feels people think she is a terrorist._

   c. _Mrs. Chan felt that being locked in at Angel Island was like_
   _being in prison._

2. It is difficult to get along in a friendly way with others around me.

   a. _____

   b. _____

   c. _____

3. I want to do something to make people around me understand me better.

   a. _____

   b. _____

   c. _____

4. I feel angry with people who express discrimination.

   a. _____

   b. _____

   c. _____

## Prisoners Without Cause

1    Another group of immigrants who were victims of unfair anti-Asian treatment were the Japanese Americans in California during World War II. These Californians, like the Chinese at Angel Island, were suddenly and unexpectedly made prisoners when they presented no problem to anyone.

2    In the years just before World War II, discrimination against Asian Americans was part of everyday life on the American West Coast. Discrimination in housing, employment, education, and every other aspect of life was common. At the same time, U.S. relations with Japan had steadily worsened. Moreover, the media constantly reinforced negative stereotypes of the Japanese as troublemakers and spies in newspapers, movies, comic strips, pulp novels,[16] and on radio.

3    As a result, it was no great surprise that when the Japanese bombed Pearl Harbor on December 7, 1941, the U.S. government within a few days arrested over 2,000 Japanese nationals in positions of leadership. No criminal charges were ever filed against them. They were imprisoned simply because of their race and their position. These arrests occurred even though the intelligence reports of the Federal Bureau of Investigation (FBI) certified that the Japanese American population presented no threat to national security.

4    The process continued over the next four years with the incarceration[17] of 92,785 Californians of Japanese ancestry in twenty-six internment[18] camps. This internment removed an entire population of hard-working Californians from public life. This had a major effect on the military, political, and economic activities

[16] *pulp novels:* cheap publications containing information intended to shock or disgust the reader
[17] *incarceration:* imprisonment, confinement
[18] *internment:* confinement

of the state at the time. Worst of all, great numbers of U.S. citizens and lawful permanent residents were imprisoned without charges, without evidence, without trial, and against every constitutional right.

5    This event remains a major embarrassment in American history that no apology can erase. Clearly Executive Order 9066 had the sole purpose of removing and imprisoning Japanese Americans at a time when German Americans and Italian Americans were equally as much, or as little, the enemies of the United States. The internment of Japanese Americans was a destructive as well as unforgivable act of discrimination. Let us hope that history does not repeat itself.

## Composition Analysis

**A Narrative Essay**   In a **narrative essay**, the writer tells a story with a purpose. The purpose is to connect the story to a truth or theme present in human nature, such as "The desire for freedom is universal." In order for the reader to understand this connection, the writer may give necessary historical background or explanation as in Reading 3, the narrative essay "Prisoners Without Cause."

This essay tells a story about the treatment of Japanese Americans in California in 1941. The author's purpose is to show that this kind of treatment is unfair and discriminatory. To convince the reader, the writer uses historical facts and explanations. These historical facts provide specific details about relevant events and the explanations provide reasons or results of the events. For example:

Historical Fact

… when the Japanese bombed Pearl Harbor on December 7, 1941, the U.S. government within a few days arrested over 2,000 Japanese nationals in positions of leadership.

Explanation

[The 2,000 Japanese nationals] were imprisoned simply because of their race and their position.

ACTIVITY 18    In Reading 3, find two examples of historical fact and two examples of explanation that support the writer's purpose. Then answer the final question.

1. **Historical Fact:**

_____

_____

**Explanation:**

_____

_____

2. **Historical Fact:**

_____

_____

**Explanation:**

_____

_____

3. What general truth about human life do these examples provide?

_____

_____

# *Writing 2*

**ACTIVITY 19** To help you prepare for the writing assignment in the next section, choose a topic and discuss the questions with a partner who has chosen the same topic as you. Write answers to the questions in your own words. You do not need to agree with your partner as long as you can give reasons for your answers.

Topic 1

1. How was the treatment of the Angel Island detainees and the Japanese internees similar?

2. How did these two groups respond?

Topic 2

1. Tell your partner a story about a time when you feel you were treated unfairly because of the attitude of someone or some group.

2. How did you feel?

**ACTIVITY 20** **Writing Assignment** Write a narrative composition about one of the following topics. Be sure to include in your paper all of the items in the checklist on page 52. You may wish to think back to some of your answers in Activity 12.

Topic 1

What two or three kinds of discrimination did both the Angel Island detainees and the Japanese internees in California experience? What were the effects of these actions on these two groups of people? How did they respond?

Topic 2

Write a narrative composition about a situation that you have experienced which seemed difficult or unfair because of the way someone or some group treated you.

# Grammar

<table>
<tr>
<td>Passive Voice</td>
<td>

**Passive** sentences and active sentences often have the same meaning, but the focus is different.

> *Active:* Today many tourists **visit** Angel Island.
> *Passive:* Today Angel Island **is visited** by many tourists.

The focus of a sentence is always its subject. In the active sentence, the focus is on tourists. In the passive sentence, the focus is on Angel Island. Writers often use passive sentences when the action or event is more important than the doer of the action.

> For the first time in American history, immigration into the United States **was refused** on the basis of race and class.

In this sentence, the important idea is the refusal of immigration, not what particular person or group of people decided on this policy.

To form a passive sentence, use a form of the verb *to be* + **the past participle** of the main verb, for example, *is visited* or *was refused*.

</td>
</tr>
</table>

**ACTIVITY 21**   For each of the following sentences, write **A** if the sentence is active or **P** if it is passive.

1. _____ By the early 1870s, when the Gold Rush had ended, the U.S. economy was slowing down.

2. _____ One of the many acts of discrimination during this time was the detention of Chinese immigrants at Angel Island in the San Francisco Bay from 1910–1940.

3. _____ Laws were passed attacking the livelihoods and civil rights of Chinese immigrants.

4. _____ The Chinese Exclusion Act was passed in 1882.

5. _____ No criminal charges were ever filed against the 92,785 Japanese internees.

6. _____ They were imprisoned simply because of their race and their position.

7. _____ Great numbers of U.S. citizens and lawful permanent residents were imprisoned without charges, without evidence, without trial, and against every constitutional right.

8. _____ Japanese Americans in California were suddenly and unexpectedly made prisoners when they presented no problem to anyone.

9. _____ Discrimination in housing, employment, education, and every other aspect of life was common.

10. _____ Immigrants were detained for weeks, months, sometimes even years.

**ACTIVITY 22** For each of the following passive sentences, write **C** if the sentence is correct or **IC** if the sentence is incorrect. If the sentence is incorrect, correct it.

1. _____ In the early 1850s, the Chinese were welcomed in the United States.

2. _____ They were values for their hard work and dedication in their jobs.

3. _____ But beginning in the early 1870s, they were treatment with racism and hatred.

4. _____ Discriminatory laws put into place that made it difficult for the Chinese to make a living.

5. _____ In 1882, a law was passed to keep more Chinese from immigrating.

6. _____ Interrogation at the Angel Island detention center was one more injustice the Chinese were force to face.

7. _____ Overall the lives of the Chinese were filled with difficulties and they were give few choices.

8. _____ The history of Chinese immigration cannot be told without giving much attention to discrimination.

## Rewriting 2

**ACTIVITY 23** **Peer Activity** Trade your paper from Activity 20 with another student. Read your partner's paper and underline the topic sentence. If your partner wrote about Topic 1, briefly describe the kinds of discrimination that both groups of people experienced. If your partner wrote about Topic 2, briefly describe the situation that seemed difficult or unfair. Then help your partner make any changes that would clarify his or her main points.

**ACTIVITY 24** **On Your Own** Review your partner's notes, your partner's comments, and your teacher's feedback on the first draft of your composition. Use the Composition Evaluation Sheet (from Appendix 1) that your teacher returned to you to see specifically what you need to improve. Then consider the questions in the checklist below. Finally, rewrite your paper to make it clearer and more meaningful.

---

**✓ CHECKLIST**

**Content**

Do you stay focused on the point of view?

Do you have any sentences that do not connect to your topic?

**Organization**

Do you have a topic sentence?

Does your topic sentence have a controlling idea?

Do you have details and examples to support your topic sentence?

Do your points follow a logical order?

Do you have a conclusion that restates the main idea in the topic sentence?

**Grammar**

Do you use the simple past and present perfect verb tenses correctly?

Do you use passive sentences correctly?

---

## Internet Activities

For additional activities related to this chapter, go to elt.thomson.com/catalyst.

# CHAPTER

# 3 Bridging the Gap Through Athletics

## Exploring the Topic

### ACTIVITY 1

**Discussion** Many people find sports attractive because they are a great "equalizer." All competitors play by the same rules and compete under the same conditions. The only way to win is to play the best. Seeing someone win against a powerful opponent or physical challenge brings people together even when they may have nothing else in common.

In groups of 3–4, discuss the following ideas and questions. Then share your ideas with the class.

1. Have you ever wanted to achieve something so much that you spent time every day for a long time to get what you wanted? What was it? Did you get what you wanted?

2. Have you ever wanted to do something that other people thought was crazy, but you did it anyway because you believed in it? What was it?

3. Have you ever been very excited about something another person was working hard to achieve? What was it? Did you do something to help this person?

53

## Reading 1: Personal Experience Reading

**Big Diomede and Little Diomede Islands**

This is the story of an athlete with a bigger purpose. The powerful opponents facing swimmer Lynne Cox were not other athletes, they were a complex Soviet[1] system, the challenge of getting sponsorship, and a narrow strait[2] of icy water separating two very different countries.

As you read the story, think about what motivates Lynne Cox to do what she does in this story. You will use your thoughts later in this chapter.

## The Bering Strait Swim

1    *In August of 1987, an American named Lynne Cox swam the 2.7 miles of frigid (5° C) water across the Bering Strait between the United States and the Soviet Union in 2 hours and 6 minutes. Her purpose was to bring the two countries closer together. This gesture of goodwill was the result of eleven years of effort to get permission to land on the Soviet shore and to raise the necessary funds[3] for the project.*

2    At the beginning of 1987, I realized I could spend the rest of my life trying to get Soviet permission to do the Bering Strait swim and to get sponsorship. I had spent eleven years writing letters and making phone calls to people in both the United States and the Soviet Union. In addition, I had to train for the swim physically, and to prepare mentally. I knew I had to set a deadline. Based on weather conditions, I decided to attempt the swim in August 1987.

3    By April, there was nothing to suggest that the Soviet support would come through. However, I had a team of people helping me so I was beginning to get

[1] *Soviet:* relating to the former Soviet Union
[2] *strait:* a narrow channel of water joining two larger bodies of water
[3] *funds:* money, resources

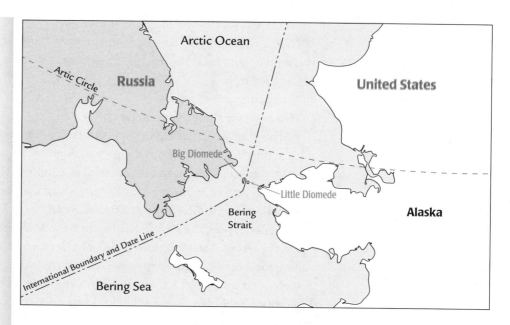

responses to my letters and phone calls. Besides permission, I also needed to find a way to pay for everything. For years I had tried to get sponsorship from large U.S. corporations, but I'd had no luck. Didn't they know what it would mean to open a market with 286 million Soviets? And maybe through this swim, not only American products could pass through Soviet borders, but also American ideas. Maybe this could be a way to help bridge the distance between the two countries.

4     In the middle of June, I decided to leave for Alaska. I had some sponsorship from local companies and individuals and this was helpful, but it wasn't nearly enough. I had to ask myself, *How can anyone believe in me unless I believe in myself?* I decided to empty out my own bank account. That, along with the contributions, would pay for my support crew's transportation, the rental house, food, phone calls, a helicopter[4] (at the group rate), and the support boats (at a reasonable cost). Unfortunately, I didn't have enough to pay for my own plane ticket. I couldn't take out a loan from the bank, so I took one out from my parents. All of this was hard; it took everything I had, emotionally, physically, and financially.

5     After a terrifying helicopter ride in heavy wind to Little Diomede, the Alaskan island where my swim would begin, I got my first look at the Bering Sea. I was horrified. It was rougher than any ocean I had ever seen. It was rougher than anything I had ever dreamed of. *It can't be like this*, I thought. *How is this ever going to work?* Staring across at Big Diomede, the Soviet island where my swim would end, I thought, *That island is only 2.7 miles from us, but it might as well be a million.* At that moment, I felt farther from the crossing than I had in eleven years.

6     Just then a teenage girl in a red parka with long brown hair and large brown eyes came over to me and said, "We are very close neighbors with the Soviets. I hope some day we can be friends with them. That has been my dream for many years." It was as if she was the voice of the child within me from so many years ago. It was as if she had come to remind me of why I was there. I had to remind myself that so many things had seemed impossible so many times. I had to change my thinking. If I didn't try, everything would be lost. I couldn't stand that thought.

[4] *helicopter:* an aircraft that can take off and land vertically

"Is the weather always like this?" I asked her.

"No, it changes every day, sometimes every twenty minutes. Sometimes the water is even flat," she said reassuringly. Then she asked me if I was really going to swim across the Strait.

"I'm going to try," I said.

"No one here thinks you can do it. But I do," she said.

7    By this time, two Alaskan newspapers, the *Nome Nugget* and *Anchorage Daily News*, were doing daily stories about the preparation for the swim. It felt like a wave of interest was building around us and with it, support. Then CNN, NBC, and NHK from Japan arrived to do stories. CKO from Canada, the BBC from Britain, and ABC radio called for live radio interviews. Reuters, the *Long Beach Press Telegram*, the *New York Times*, the *Philadelphia Inquirer*, the *Manchester Union Leader*, the *Boston Globe*, the *Orange County Register*, the *Chicago Tribune*, and so many others were calling for interviews. All of the journalists were asking the same question: Will the Soviets open the border for you and allow you to swim? Trying to sound positive, I told them I thought they would, but I had no idea if they would really do it.

*(continued in Reading 2)*

Excerpt from the book, *Swimming to Antarctica,* by Lynne Cox.

---

**ACTIVITY 2**    Discuss these questions with your classmates. You may wish to take some notes for use later in Activity 6.

1. Why did Lynne Cox want to swim across the Bering Strait?

2. How long did she try to get permission from the Soviets to do the swim? Does this surprise you?

3. What did she finally decide to do after trying for many years to get permission? Why do you think she did this?

4. How did she raise all the money to do the swim?

5. How did the Bering Strait look to her when she first saw it? How did this make her feel about her swim?

6. What two things happened that added to her confidence that she could do the swim?

7. Why did these two things make her feel better?

## Vocabulary

**ACTIVITY 3**    **Academic Words** Choose the correct word to fill each blank in the sentences below.

| Words | Meanings |
|---|---|
| **contribution** | payment made for a specific purpose |
| **corporation** | an organization formed for business |

| | |
|---|---|
| **financially** | having to do with money |
| **individual** | a single human as part of a group |
| **irresistible** | very desirable |
| **mentally** | relating to the mind |
| **opponent** | one that takes the opposite side or position |
| **physically** | relating to the body |
| **positively** | with good feeling, optimistic |
| **project** | a task that requires a lot of effort |
| **response** | an answer |
| **team** | a group of people working together for a common purpose |
| **terrifying** | deeply frightening |
| **transportation** | a means of moving |

1. The Bering Strait swim was a _____ so huge that it took more than eleven years.

   a. project          b. corporation

2. Lynne Cox needed _____ to get to the tiny island of Little Diomede where the swim would begin.

   a. transportation     b. a response

3. In addition to training for the swim _____ Cox needed to believe in herself to prepare mentally.

   a. physically          b. positively

4. Nature herself is often a stronger _____ than human beings.

   a. opponent          b. team

5. Lynne Cox spent many years trying to get _____ from major corporations so that she could cover the costs of her swim.

   a. individuals        b. contributions

6. People who find chocolate _____ may be surprised to learn that it can actually make you feel better mentally.

   a. terrifying          b. irresistible

7. In addition to preparing her mind and body for the swim, Cox had to prepare _____ so she could cover the costs of the swim.

   a. mentally          b. financially

# Composition Analysis

**Thesis Statements in Essays** An **essay** is a piece of writing of more than one or two paragraphs with a specific purpose. The purpose is to persuade the reader of the writer's point of view about the topic. The format of an essay includes three parts: an **introductory paragraph**, a **body**, and a **concluding paragraph**.

The **introductory paragraph** captures the reader's interest and gives general information and background about the topic. The last sentence of the paragraph is the **thesis statement**. It gives the writer's point of view and the specific focus on the topic of the essay.

The **body** may contain one or more paragraphs that explain the thesis statement and give details and examples to support it. This is the part of the essay where the writer does the main work of persuading the reader. It usually consists of two or more main points supported by details. Or it may tell a story that communicates a certain truth or teaches a lesson.

The **concluding paragraph** restates or summarizes the main idea of the thesis statement. It may also leave the reader with something to think about or make a prediction about the future.

The **thesis statement** most importantly tells the writer's attitude or opinion about the topic. It also predicts what aspects of the topic the writer will discuss. The thesis statement is not just a statement of fact and it does not just announce a general topic. It provides for an essay what a topic sentence provides for a paragraph. Look at the following sentences:

A  Participation in athletics can teach children skills that will be useful to them in other areas of their lives.

This is an effective thesis statement because it tells the writer's point of view about the topic, which is that children can learn useful skills from playing a sport. It also narrows the topic and lets the reader know what to expect. The reader knows, for example, that the essay will not be about the risk of injury in athletics, or about the procedure for starting a child in athletics.

B  I would like to write about children participating in athletics.

This is *not* an effective thesis statement because it does not give a point of view, does not focus the topic, and does not predict how the essay will handle the topic. Unlike sentence A, the reader does not know if the essay will be about the expense, the time commitment, or anything else in particular about children participating in athletics.

C  Children are better off if they participate in athletics.

This is *not* an effective thesis statement. It does have a point of view, but, unlike sentence A, it does not have a specific focus and the reader does not know why children are better off if they participate in athletics.

D  Participation in athletics is a wonderful experience for a child.

This is *not* an effective thesis statement. It does not have a specific focus because "wonderful" is a very general term. Therefore the reader knows only that the writer believes that participation in athletics is positive, but nothing about why.

Circle the letter of the best thesis statement. Then give a reason for your answer.

1. a. People will remember Lynne Cox's swims for a long time because of the messages of goodwill they carry.

   b. I would like to write about Lynne Cox, who swims in water cold enough to kill most people.

   **Reason:** _____

   _____

2. a. The Bering Strait swim is only one of the many cold water swims that Lynne Cox has completed.

   b. The Bering Strait swim was Lynne Cox's most important swim because it brought people whose governments were enemies together as friends.

   **Reason:** _____

   _____

3. a. People came together out of respect and excitement for the challenge of Lynne Cox's swim.

   b. Long distance swimming events are a good way to bring people together.

   **Reason:** _____

   _____

4. a. Two difficult challenges that Lynne Cox faced were getting permission and raising money.

   b. For Lynne Cox, getting permission and raising money took even more determination than swimming across the Bering Strait.

   **Reason:** _____

   _____

5. a. Lynne Cox has become known the world over for her cold and difficult swims.

   b. Lynne Cox has won the hearts of people around the world with her cold swims and warm spirit.

   **Reason:** _____

   _____

**ACTIVITY 5** To help you prepare for the writing assignment in Activity 6, choose a topic and discuss the questions with a partner who has chosen the same topic as you. Write answers to the questions in your own words. You do not need to agree with your partner as long as you can give reasons for your answers.

## Topic 1

1. What difficulties did Lynne Cox have to deal with during the time leading up to the swim?

2. Do you think these challenges contributed to her desire to succeed?

3. Why was her desire to do the swim so strong?

## Topic 2

1. Tell your partner about a time you or someone you know did something especially challenging to help someone.

2. Why was it so important to do this?

**ACTIVITY 6** **Writing Assignment** Write a composition about one of the following topics. Be sure to include in your paper all of the items in the checklist on page 63. Try to begin with a thesis statement and include each supporting point in a new paragraph.

## Topic 1

Describe the challenges that Lynne Cox faces that contribute to her strong desire for success. Think about why she wanted to do the swim and what she needed in order to do it.

## Topic 2

Describe a time when you or someone you know did something very difficult or dangerous in order to help someone else. Think about the reasons you did this and the steps you went through to accomplish what you wanted.

# Grammar

**Transition Words and Phrases**

**Transition words and phrases** contribute to the overall flow, or cohesion, of a composition. They also contribute to the meaning by showing relationships between ideas. Many transitions make use of a dependent phrase followed by an independent clause. Often the transition phrase begins a sentence. Look at the following transition words in **boldface** used in sentences from Reading 1.

| Transitions Showing Time | Meaning |
|---|---|
| **At that moment** I felt farther from the crossing than I had in eleven years. | At a certain point in time |
| **Just then** a teenage girl in a red parka with long brown hair and large brown eyes came over to me and said, "We are very close neighbors with the Soviets. ... " | At that time |
| **By this time**, two Alaskan newspapers, the *Nome Nugget* and *Anchorage Daily News*, were doing daily stories about the preparation for the swim. | Going on at the present time |

| Other Transitions | Meaning |
|---|---|
| **In addition** [to writing letters and making phone calls to get permission to do the Bering Strait swim], I had to train for the swim physically, and to prepare mentally. | Plus |
| **Unfortunately**, I didn't have enough to pay for my own plane ticket. | Too bad |

**Connecting prepositions** followed by noun phrases also contribute to the flow of a composition and show relationships between ideas. Look at the following connecting prepositions in **boldface** used in sentences from Reading 1.

| Connecting Prepositions | Meaning |
|---|---|
| **After** a terrifying helicopter ride in heavy wind to Little Diomede, the Alaskan island where my swim would begin, I got my first look at the Bering Sea. | Following |
| **Based on** weather conditions, I decided to attempt the swim in August 1987. | Because of |
| **Besides** permission, I also needed to find a way to pay for everything. | In addition to |

**ACTIVITY 7**  Fill the blanks in the following sentences with a word or phrase from the list. Do not add any other words. Some sentences have more than one correct answer.

at that moment          by this time          unfortunately
just then               in addition

1. I sat down to eat dinner and took my first bite. _____ the doorbell rang.

2. _____ my car broke down so I will be unable to go to the mountains for the weekend. I am very disappointed.

3. We have most of our belongings packed up. _____ next week, we will be completely moved in and living in our new house.

4. I have two papers to write and one exam to take this week. _____ I need to take care of my son who is very sick. I just don't know how I'll get everything done.

5. After my flight, I was waiting for my baggage by the carousel. _____ I saw a friend of mine that I had not seen for thirty years.

6. As I was driving down the highway, I saw a car coming toward me pull out into my lane to pass another car. _____ I wondered if I would live to reach my destination.

7. _____ to working full time, Maria is also going to school to get a degree in computer science.

**Write a sentence of your own using one of the transitions above.**

8. _____

_____

**ACTIVITY 8**  Fill the blanks in the following sentences with a preposition from the list. Do not add any other words. Some sentences have more than one correct answer.

after          based on          besides

1. _____ the most recent figures, our company made a larger than expected profit this quarter.

2. _____ paying for her own plane ticket to Alaska, Lynne Cox had to cover the transportation costs for her crew.

3. _____ his final exams were over, Juan felt completely exhausted.

4. _____ the wet weather today, I suggest we cancel the picnic.

Write a sentence of your own using one of the prepositions above.

5. _____

_____

## Rewriting 1

ACTIVITY 9

**Peer Activity** Trade your paper from Activity 6 with another student. Read your partner's paper and underline the thesis statement. If you can't find a thesis statement, see if you can help your partner write one. Next, underline the topic sentence of each body paragraph and put a circle around each controlling idea. If you can't find any of the topic sentences, see if you can help your partner write the ones that are missing. Talk to your partner about what you found and help him or her make any necessary changes.

ACTIVITY 10

**On Your Own** Review your partner's notes, your partner's comments, and your teacher's feedback on the first draft of your composition. Use the Composition Evaluation Sheet (from Appendix 1) that your teacher returned to you to see specifically what you need to improve. Then consider the questions in the checklist below. Finally, rewrite your paper to make it clearer and more meaningful.

✓CHECKLIST

Content

Topic 1: Do you clearly show the challenges Lynne Cox faces?

Topic 2: Do you clearly show why you wanted to help someone else?

Do you have one or more support paragraphs?

Do you have a conclusion?

Organization

Do you have a thesis statement that clearly states the purpose and point of view of your composition?

Does each support paragraph have a topic sentence?

Does each topic sentence have a controlling idea?

Does each topic sentence connect to the thesis statement?

Grammar

Do you use verb tenses correctly?

Do you use transition words and phrases correctly?

## *Reading 2:* Extending the Topic Reading

**Little Diomede: Starting Point of the Bering Strait Swim**

For Lynne Cox, the long struggle with her opponents at last makes way for the sweetness of success.

As you read this part of the story, think about the different ways that Lynne Cox is achieving success for herself and others. You will use your thoughts later in this chapter.

8　　One day before my proposed swim date, I just couldn't understand why we hadn't heard from the Soviets. I was especially worried because someone had seen through a telescope[5] that the Soviets had moved two ships the size of football fields just a mile south of Big Diomede and all day they had been posting guards around the island and off-loading men, guns, and equipment. Something was going on and no one knew what it was.

9　　Suddenly one of the reporters ran in and grabbed me by the arm and told me that David Karp, who was in charge of handling communications for me, was on the phone from Moscow. "He has heard from the Soviets. Come on, hurry, run! Hurry, he might get disconnected. He's been trying to reach you all night, but he couldn't get through," she said. I nervously picked up the phone. He was crying. He tried to talk, but he couldn't get the words out.

*Oh, no, no, no!* my mind screamed. *After all this the Soviets have said no.* I waited forever for the weight of his words. My heart was about to burst into a million pieces.

[5] *telescope:* an instrument for viewing faraway places or things

His voice finally came through. "The Soviets said yes. Yes! You can do it." He was crying again.

10     All at once it was as if all the pressure of uncertainty had changed into energy. The doctors eagerly checked and packed their equipment. The journalists dictated stories, and the photographers snapped what seemed like hundreds of pictures.

11     At last, on the day of my swim, with my heart pounding in my chest, I hit the icy water with a splash. I began stroking as fast as my arms would turn over. Nothing had ever felt as good as that moment. Finally I was swimming across the Bering Strait from the United States to the Soviet Union. My strokes—what I could feel with numb[6] arms—were strong and powerful. The sea was calm, but I felt full of energy, excitement, and happiness. I was living my dream that so many people were sharing with me.

12     After more than two hours in the frigid water and thick fog, I needed both hands to crawl[7] out of the sea. I tried to move forward, but I slid backward. I stepped up. Three men were leaning toward me, extending their arms as far as they could. They were smiling and shouting in Russian. I leaned forward and reached as high as I could. I felt the warmth of their hands in mine. Then one man draped his coat over my shoulders and a woman piled blankets over me. Another man was kissing me all over my face. I was shivering and I could hardly walk. I knew my body temperature was dropping, but I wanted to meet everyone there, to see their faces, to see real live Russians—people I had been afraid of all my life. It was so strange; they were all smiling, all excited, all thrilled to be there.

13     One Inuit[8] woman, a pediatrician[9] from Magadan, kissed me on both cheeks and gave me a bouquet[10] of wildflowers from her village on the Siberian mainland. I kissed her the same way and she told me, fighting to hold tears back, that she had family living on both sides of the Bering Strait, on Little Diomede and on Big Diomede. However, they had been separated by political differences that none of them believed in. She told me that after today she thought they might see each other again; maybe this was the beginning. She smiled and her eyes filled with tears. Mine did too, and I just had to hug her again and say, "Yes, someday this will happen, I just know it."

14     The Soviets had sent more than fifty people to welcome us with open arms, as if we were long-lost friends. On the rocky beach they set up two large tables covered with white tablecloths where waiters served hot tea in china cups, dried fish, bread, and chocolate-covered coconut candy. There were people standing around the tables, Americans and Soviets, just talking. On Pat Omiak's two-way radio we could hear someone on Little Diomede singing. Then the whole village joined in. They were singing Siberian (Russian) Yupik songs. Some of the Inuits on Big Diomede joined in; these were the songs they had learned as children. As they sang back and forth to each other, some of the villagers started doing traditional Inuit dances. The gap created by all the years of separation was closing.

15     Four months later, we saw on television the first history-making meeting at the White House between President Reagan and President Gorbachev. They were

---

[6] *numb:* without feeling
[7] *crawl:* move slowly using hands and feet
[8] *Inuit:* a group of Eskimoan people living in the Arctic
[9] *pediatrician:* a physician who specializes in children and infants
[10] *bouquet:* an arrangement of flowers

signing the INF Missile Treaty. This meant that both countries were going to start reducing their supply of nuclear arms.[11] President Gorbachev made a toast[12] and said, "Last summer it took one brave American by the name of Lynne Cox just two hours to swim from one of our countries to the other. We saw on television how sincere and friendly the meeting was between our people and the Americans when she stepped onto the Soviet shore. She proved by her courage how close to each other our peoples live." Later he added that he saw the swim as a symbol of improving relations between the United States and the Soviet Union.

[11] *nuclear arms:* atomic weapons of war
[12] *toast:* drink honoring an event or accomplishment

**ACTIVITY 11**

**A. Discussion** Discuss these questions with your classmates.

1. What happened that Cox worried about the day before her swim?

2. When Cox got the phone call from David Karp, did she expect to hear good news? How do you know?

3. Why was he crying?

4. How did Cox's feelings change after the phone call?

5. What did she mean when she said, "I was living my dream that so many people were sharing with me"?

**B.** Read the following quote and answer questions 6–8. You may wish to take some notes to use later in Activity 18.

Immediately following her Bering Strait swim, the Soviet press asked Cox why she made the swim and how she felt about it. This is what she said: "The reason I swam across the Bering Strait was to reach into the future and to bridge the distance between the United States and the Soviet Union. It was to create goodwill and peace between our two countries, our two peoples. I would not have swum here if I believed that the Soviet Union was an evil empire.[13] I can't say if the swim will contribute to the reduction of the nuclear weapons, but I sure hope it does. We need to become friends. That is why I did this; that is why my team did this."

[13] *evil empire:* a country with harmful intentions

6. Why do you think both Soviet and American people responded to the Bering Strait swim?

7. Why do you think the Soviets decided to give Cox their permission?

8. Write three things you think people admire about Lynne Cox.

a. _____

b. _____

c. _____

**Group Activity** In a group of 3–4 students, make a list of events that happened during and after the Bering Strait swim that opened communication between the Soviets and the Americans. Try to find at least five events from Reading 2. Discuss in your group why you think each event improved the relationship between Soviets and Americans. Present your list and your reasons to the class. The first one is done for you.

1. **Event:** _Three [Soviet] men were leaning toward me, extending their arms as far as they could. They were smiling and shouting in Russian._

   **Reason:** _The Soviet men offered Cox friendly help._

2. **Event:** _____

   _____

   **Reason:** _____

   _____

3. **Event:** _____

   _____

   **Reason:** _____

   _____

4. **Event:** _____

   _____

   **Reason:** _____

   _____

5. **Event:** _____

   _____

   **Reason:** _____

   _____

6. **Event:** _____

   _____

   **Reason:** _____

   _____

# Vocabulary

**Academic Words** Write the letter of the correct definition in the blank.

1. _____ created
2. _____ shivering
3. _____ thrilled
4. _____ symbol
5. _____ pressure
6. _____ pounding
7. _____ courage
8. _____ equipment
9. _____ traditional
10. _____ energy

a. the power to do physical work
b. repeated heavy beating
c. made
d. the weight of worry about something unavoidable
e. related to a time-honored practice
f. something that represents by association something else
g. bravery to face something dangerous or difficult
h. items needed to perform a task
i. shaking with cold
j. very excited

# Composition Analysis

**Transitions Showing Time** As you learned earlier in this chapter, transition words and phrases contribute to the overall flow of a composition. They also contribute to the meaning by showing relationships between ideas. Here are more transition words and phrases in **boldface** that are from Reading 1.

| Transitions Showing Time | Meaning |
| --- | --- |
| **Suddenly** one of the reporters ran in and grabbed me by the arm and told me that David Karp was on the phone. | Coming unexpectedly |
| **All at once** it was as if all the pressure of uncertainty had changed into energy. | Coming without warning |
| **At last** on the day of my swim, with my heart pounding in my chest, I hit the icy water with a splash. | At the end |
| **Finally** I was swimming across the Bering Strait from the United States to the Soviet Union. | In the end |
| On Pat Omiak's two-way radio we could hear someone on Little Diomede singing. **Then** the whole village joined in. | Next |
| **Later** he added that he saw the swim as a symbol of improving relations between the United States and the Soviet Union. | After a time |

**ACTIVITY 14**   Fill the blanks in the following sentences with a transition word or phrase from the list. Some sentences have more than one correct answer.

| | | |
|---|---|---|
| suddenly | at last | then |
| all at once | finally | later |

1. I thought my cold would never end. _____, after a whole month it went away.

2. I was sitting quietly drinking my coffee and reading the paper. _____ the ground began to shake. I knew immediately it was an earthquake.

3. Lynne Cox waited eleven years to get permission from the Soviets. _____, just when she thought she would never hear from them, she got a phone call.

4. First I went to buy some flowers. _____ I went to visit my friend in the hospital.

5. _____, long after all the celebration was over, Cox would think about the importance of what she had accomplished.

6. _____, with the help of her team of supporters, Cox was able to go ahead with her swim.

7. _____, after many years of research, he was able to complete his book.

## Making Connections

**Description** is used in an essay to tell what something is like. A writer may describe a person, a place, an event, or an idea. The writer uses specific concrete details to create a clear picture in the reader's mind. Description is often used in an essay together with other methods of presentation such as narration, definition, or process.

   Notice that paragraph 1 of Reading 1 gives an overview of the event that the reading is about and all of the other paragraphs in Readings 1 and 2 give a description of the specific details that make the event come alive. The writer describes different aspects of the event, including the purpose of the Bering Strait Swim, the process of getting permission, the process of getting sponsorship, and the mental preparation. In the description of these aspects, the writer uses at least three kinds of description—words that appeal to the senses, description that creates a clear mental picture, and description that communicates an important feeling. Look at the following examples.

Example 1

   **The purpose of the Bering Strait swim** (Reading 2, paragraph 14) (The purpose was to bring the two countries closer together.)

   **Words that appeal to the senses:** On the rocky beach [at the end of the swim, the Soviets] set up two large tables covered with **white tablecloths** where waiters served **hot tea** in **china cups**, **dried fish**, bread, and **chocolate-covered coconut candy**. (Notice the words in **boldface** that appeal to the sense of sight, touch, smell, and taste.)

**Description that creates a clear mental picture:** There were people standing around the tables, Americans and Soviets, just talking.

**Description that communicates an important feeling:** [The Inuits on Little Diomede] were singing Siberian (Russian) Yupik songs [on the two-way radio]. Some of the Inuits on Big Diomede joined in; these were the songs they had learned as children. As they sang back and forth to each other, some of the villagers started doing traditional Inuit dances.

Example 2

**The mental preparation for the Bering Strait swim** (Reading 1, paragraph 6) (Lynne Cox was discouraged by the roughness of the Bering Sea.)

**Words that appeal to the senses:** Just then a teenage girl in a **red parka** with **long brown hair** and **large brown eyes** came over to me. (Notice the words in **boldface** that appeal to the sense of sight.)

**Description that communicates an important feeling:** [The girl in the red parka] said, "We are very close neighbors with the Soviets. I hope some day we can be friends with them. That has been my dream for many years." … It was as if she had come to remind me of why I was there.

ACTIVITY 15 · Find several sentences that provide description for each of the following aspects of the Bering Strait swim. Then tell which reading and paragraph your example came from. Write the sentences next to the correct kind of description. You may not find all three kinds of description for each example.

1. The process of trying to get permission for the swim (Reading _____,

   paragraph _____)

   **Words that appeal to the senses:** _____

   _____

   _____

   **Description that creates a clear mental picture:** _____

   _____

   _____

   **Description that communicates an important feeling:** _____

   _____

   _____

2. The process of trying to get sponsorship for the swim (Reading _____,
   paragraph _____)

   **Words that appeal to the senses:** _____

   _____

   _____

   **Description that creates a clear mental picture:** _____

   _____

   _____

   **Description that communicates an important feeling:** _____

   _____

   _____

3. The process of receiving permission for the swim (Reading _____,
   paragraph _____)

   **Words that appeal to the senses:** _____

   _____

   _____

   **Description that creates a clear mental picture:** _____

   _____

   _____

   **Description that communicates an important feeling:** _____

   _____

   _____

**Jackie Robinson**

## Breaking Barriers Through Athletics

1    The idea of holding athletic events to ease political differences and close cultural gaps is not a new one. At key moments in American history, athletic competitions, which emphasize equality and fairness, have helped to break barriers between people.

2    The game of baseball, for example, has broken many social barriers. In 1947, when African Americans were still excluded from playing major league baseball, Jackie Robinson became the first black player to receive a major league baseball contract. His first few games made front-page headlines, which marked the beginning of his acceptance as a baseball player. Still he was most often turned away at the hotels and restaurants his white teammates used. That same year he made "Rookie of the Year." Then, in 1954, the nearly seventy-year-old "separate but equal" law finally ended and segregation[14] became illegal.

3    Another "first" for baseball was the formation of a women's league from 1943–1954. The league began during World War II when patriotism[15] was strong and large numbers of young men were overseas fighting for their country. At the beginning of each game, the players stood in the formation of a "V" for Victory (in the war) followed by the playing of the Star Spangled Banner.[16] Players also

[14] *segregation:* the practice of separating people of different races
[15] *patriotism:* love of country and willingness to fight for it
[16] *Star Spangled Banner:* the American national anthem

participated in exhibition[17] games to support the Red Cross and the armed forces and visited wounded veterans[18] at Army hospitals. These actions made the women's league very popular, but they put women in roles that were non-traditional at the time.

4    In 1985, Ted Turner attempted to break a different kind of barrier. In 1984, the Soviet Union had boycotted[19] the Summer Olympics in Los Angeles so he decided to organize an Olympic-style competition between the United States and the Soviet Union in Moscow. The first so-called Goodwill Games were held in 1986 and got good media coverage. Because of the success of the 1986 games, they were continued in Seattle in 1990, St. Petersburg in 1994, and again in New York in 1998. In 2000, a Winter Goodwill Games was held in Lake Placid, New York, which included 442 athletes from 22 countries. The fifth Goodwill Games, for the first time held outside the United States or the former U.S.S.R., were in Brisbane, Australia, in 2001. The long-standing success of these games was a clear celebration of goodwill.

5    In conclusion, athletic competitions, because of the public attention they draw to equality for all, provide an excellent opportunity for breaking many kinds of barriers.

[17] *exhibition:* games to raise money for a cause
[18] *veteran:* a soldier who has ended military service
[19] *boycott:* refuse to participate

# Composition Analysis

**A Descriptive Essay** The following paragraph is a shorter one-paragraph version of the essay in Reading 3. Notice that the paragraph and the essay cover the same points, but the essay has many more descriptive details.

At key moments in American history, athletic competitions, which emphasize equality and fairness, have helped break barriers between people. For example, in 1947 Jackie Robinson was the first black player to receive a major league baseball contract—at a time when African Americans were still excluded from playing major league baseball. The same year he made "Rookie of the Year." Then, in 1954, segregation became illegal after nearly seventy years. A second example from baseball was the existence of a women's league from 1943–1954. These women contributed much to patriotism by playing additional exhibition games to support the Red Cross and the armed forces and by visiting wounded veterans in Army hospitals. The league became very popular while it showed women in new roles. Again in 1985, Ted Turner attempted to break a barrier by organizing the Goodwill Games in response to the Soviet boycott of the Summer Olympics in Los Angeles. Five Goodwill Games were held between 1986 and 2001. The long-standing success of these games was a clear celebration of goodwill. In conclusion, athletic competitions, because of the public attention they draw to equality for all, provide an excellent opportunity for breaking barriers of many kinds.

**ACTIVITY 16**

**A.** Underline the topic sentences of the paragraphs in the essay in Reading 3. Next underline the sentences in the paragraph above that are the same or nearly the same as the topic sentences in the essay. Then answer the following questions.

1. What is the thesis statement of the essay? _____

   _____

   _____

2. What is the topic sentence of the paragraph? _____

   _____

   _____

3. How many main points does the writer make in the essay? _____

4. How many points does the writer make in the paragraph? _____

5. How does the writer give more detail in the essay than in the paragraph? Choose all answers that are correct.

    a. by giving more main points

    b. by giving more examples for each main point

    c. by adding more detail to the introduction

    d. by adding more detail to the conclusion

**B.** Consider the following information in answering questions 6–8.

   The essay "Breaking Barriers Through Athletics" is a **descriptive essay**. The writer's purpose is to explain the role of athletics in breaking the barriers between people that are created by strongly held attitudes. The writer uses descriptive details and examples to create a clear picture of several barriers and to show the effects that athletics has on them.

6. Does the writer have a positive or a negative attitude about athletics as a way to change people's thinking? _____ Write one sentence from the essay to support your answer. _____

    _____

7. What are the three examples of breaking barriers that the writer gives? Give one detail that supports each example. The first one is done for you.

    a. **Example:** _Jackie Robinson became the first black player to receive a_
       _major league baseball contract—at a time when African Americans_
       _were still banned from playing major league baseball._

       **Detail:** _His first few games made front-page headlines, which helped_
       _him become accepted as a baseball player._

    b. **Example:** _____

       **Detail:** _____

    c. **Example:** _____

       **Detail:** _____

8. What does the writer conclude about the effects of athletics on breaking barriers?

    _____

# *Writing 2*

ACTIVITY 17 To help you prepare for the writing assignment in Activity 18, choose a topic and discuss the questions with a partner who has chosen the same topic as you. Write answers to the questions in your own words. You do not need to agree with your partner as long as you can give reasons for your answers.

Topic 1

1. What do you think attracts people about Lynne Cox's story?

2. Which details of her story do you find most interesting?

Topic 2

1. Why do you think sports and sports heroes have the power to change people's attitudes?

2. Which of the three examples in Reading 3 is the most meaningful to you? Why?

ACTIVITY 18 **Writing Assignment** Write a descriptive essay about one of the topics below. You may wish to use some of the notes you took in Activities 2 and 11. Be sure to include in your paper all of the items in the checklist on page 80.

Topic 1

Describe the three most important reasons why people found Lynne Cox's success in swimming across the Bering Strait so irresistible. Give details and examples to support your answer.

Topic 2

Describe the effect you think one of the three examples in Reading 3 had on changing people's attitudes and why you think it changed them. Give details and examples to support your answer.

**The Past Progressive and Past Perfect Verb Tenses**

The **past progressive** verb tense is used to express an activity that was going on at a particular time in the past. The activity was not complete at that particular time. The past progressive is formed with *was* or *were* + the *-ing* **form** of the main verb.

> I **was swimming** across the Bering Strait from the United States to the Soviet Union.

The activity of swimming across the Bering Strait was going on in August of 1987. It was not complete at the time the sentence refers to.

> I **was living** my dream that so many people were sharing with me.

At the time this sentence refers to, her dream was in progress and it was continuing.

> They **were signing** the INF Missile Treaty.

The signing of the treaty was going on and not complete at the time the sentence refers to.

The **past perfect** verb tense is used to express an activity that was completed before a particular identified time in the past. The past perfect is formed with *had* + the **past participle** of the main verb.

> Nothing **had** ever **felt** as good as that moment.

There was nothing as good at any time before that moment in the past.

> One day before my proposed swim date I just couldn't understand why we **had**n't **heard** from the Soviets.

For all of the time up until the day before the swim, there was no word from the Soviets.

> The Soviets **had sent** more than fifty people to welcome us with open arms, as if we were long-lost friends.

Sending fifty people was complete before the welcoming.

> Some of the Inuits on Big Diomede joined in; these were the songs they **had learned** as children.

The Inuits learned the songs (as children) before they joined in.

The important difference between the past progressive and the past perfect is what is happening at a given point in time in the past. In the past progressive, an activity is continuing and not complete. In the past perfect, the activity is complete.

Fill each blank with the past progressive or past perfect form of the verb in parentheses.

Jackie Robinson was successful at more than just baseball. By the time he made Rookie of the Year in 1947, Jackie Robinson's role in baseball (**1. draw**–*past perfect*) _____ so much attention that it (**2. become**–*past perfect*) _____ a civil rights issue. Racial attitudes which would lead to desegregation[20] of a country (**3. change**–*past progressive*) _____ on the baseball fields of America. But these changes came with a high price for Jackie Robinson. He had to play ball while pitchers[21] (**4. throw**–*past progressive*) _____ balls at his head, players (**5. cut**–*past progressive*) _____ him with their cleats,[22] and catchers (**6. spit**–*past progressive*) _____ on his shoes. After these difficult games he often left the field, only to learn that he (**7. receive**–*past perfect*) _____ hate letters and death threats in the mail while he (**8. play**–*past progressive*) _____ ball. But Jackie Robinson showed the self-control to answer these racist acts with silence. In time, his country saw that he (**9. won**–*past perfect*) _____ the respect of his teammates as well as his opponents.

[20] *desegregation:* ending the legal process of separating people based on race
[21] *pitcher:* the player on a baseball team who throws the ball for the batter to hit
[22] *cleats:* pieces of metal on the bottom of baseball shoes that provide traction for running

For each of the following sentences, write **C** if the sentence is correct and write **IC** if the sentence is incorrect. If the sentence is incorrect, correct it.

1. _____ By the time Jackie Robinson made Rookie of the Year, baseball had already begun to change.

2. _____ While large numbers of young men were serving their country during World War II, a women's baseball league played games for eleven years.

3. _____ When Lynne Cox reached the shore of Big Diomede, at least fifty Russians were prepare to welcome her.

4. _____ Because the Soviets had boycotted the Olympics in 1986, Ted Turner took the opportunity to organize the Goodwill Games.

5. _____ While Lynne Cox had hoped to get permission to do the Bering Strait swim, she kept writing letters and making phone calls.

6. _____ The Soviets had already sending boats, guns, and equipment to Big Diomede by the time Cox learned she had permission to do the swim.

7. _____ Jackie Robinson was played baseball at a time when African Americans were not permitted in the same restaurants and hotels as white Americans.

8. _____ By the time Robinson retired in 1956, he had led the way for generations of black athletes.

## Rewriting 2

ACTIVITY 21

**Peer Activity** Trade your paper from Activity 18 with another student. Read your partner's paper and underline the thesis statement. Then do one of the following:

1. If your partner wrote about Topic 1, make a list of the three reasons why people were excited about Lynne Cox's success. You do not need to write complete sentences.

2. If your partner wrote about Topic 2, make a list of the two or three effects that athletics have on changing people's attitudes. You do not need to write complete sentences.

Next, check to see if the conclusion seems like a logical result of the points you listed. Talk to your partner about what you found and help him or her make any necessary changes.

**ACTIVITY 22** | **On Your Own** Review your partner's notes, your partner's comments, and your teacher's feedback on the first draft of your composition. Use the Composition Evaluation Sheet (from Appendix 1) that your teacher returned to you to see specifically what you need to improve. Then consider the questions in the checklist below. Finally, rewrite your paper to make it clearer and more meaningful.

**CHECKLIST**

**Content**

Do you use description to address the topic?

Do you have a clear thesis statement that supports the topic?

Do you have a conclusion?

**Organization**

Do the topic sentences of your support paragraphs support your thesis statement?

Do the details and examples in your support paragraphs support their topic sentences?

Do you have any irrelevant sentences?

**Grammar**

Do you use transition words and phrases correctly?

Do you use the past progressive and past perfect verb tenses correctly?

## Internet Activities

For additional activities related to this chapter, go to elt.thomson.com/catalyst.

# CHAPTER 4

# Family Issues and Marriage

## Exploring the Topic

### ACTIVITY 1

**Discussion** Every culture has its own strong traditions on marriage. Even within one culture, people sometimes have opposing views about marriage. Some may believe in the benefits of an arranged marriage, in which the partners are brought together by a third person, while others have true faith only in a love marriage, in which the partners choose each other.

In groups of 3–4, discuss the following ideas and questions. Then share your ideas with the class.

1. Do parents often live with their married children in your parents' culture?

2. Do you think this is a good arrangement? Why or why not?

3. What do you think of the way married children live separately from their parents in the United States?

4. Who takes care of older people in your parents' culture?

5. Would you want to have an older parent living with you? Why or why not?

## Reading 1: Personal Experience Reading

This is Hiro's story. He is a university student from Japan who will soon finish his degree and get married. However, this means he has a difficult decision to make. His mother wants to come and live with the young couple after the wedding, but his fiancé³ doesn't understand this idea and is very much against it.

**As you read the story, think about what you think Hiro should do to solve his problem. You will use your thoughts later in this chapter.**

## Caught in the Middle

1    Hiro came to the United States on a student visa three and a half years ago and is studying computer science at a university. He has done well in his studies and will finish his degree in three months. When he decided to come to the United States to study, his intention was to return to Japan when he got his degree. He planned to go to work in his home country to be near his parents, relatives, and friends.

2    Now in his fourth year of school, Hiro has grown more comfortable with life in America and appreciates the greater freedom of choices and the fewer restrictions based on traditions. He has discovered that he can choose the kind of job he wants and, as long as he can afford it, he can live where he wants. He doesn't have to follow in anyone else's footsteps.⁴ He can do what he wants. He has also discovered that, in terms of salary and advancement possibilities, he could probably do much

³ *fiancé*: a man or woman who is engaged to be married
⁴ *follow in someone's footsteps*: do the same as what someone ahead of you has done

better in the United States than in Japan. In fact, he has already received one job offer to begin work at a software company after he graduates.

3    In addition to these considerations, Hiro found on his last visit home that he had less to talk about with his old friends and he felt less a part of Japanese life. He felt eager to return "home" to the United States even though the reason for his visit to Japan was because his father was dying. He stayed as long as he could, but he knew his mother wanted him to stay longer, especially because Hiro is her only child. He, however, needed to get back to school.

4    Now Hiro has become engaged to an American girl that he met at the university and he has accepted the job offer because they will need his income. He is very happy that he and Hanna will be married soon, although he is not happy that he feels he has let his mother down.[5] He knows she would prefer that he marry a girl whose family she knows. An arranged marriage like her own would be even better in his mother's view. She has never met Hanna or her family, and Hanna is not even Japanese.

5    When Hiro told his mother about his engagement and his plans to accept a job in the United States, it was very difficult for him. She was happy for him, but she was also upset. She did not like the idea that he would live so far away and she would remain with no husband and without her only son. Hiro tried to explain the situation to Hanna. However, when he told her that in Japan it is quite common for parents to live with their married children and that he wanted to ask his mother to come and live with them, they argued. Hanna, being American, is not used to the idea of living with parents after marriage. She believes that a husband and wife must find their own way and make their own decisions without interference from parents. She said it would be OK if his mother wanted to visit for a few weeks from time to time, but she refused to agree to having her live with them permanently.

6    Last night when Hiro again talked to his mother, she told him that she feels old and alone and misses him very much. Therefore, when she comes for the wedding she wants to stay and live with them. She said she could help with expenses and help take care of the grandchildren. Now Hiro must tell Hanna what his mother wants to do.

7    Hiro feels trapped. He knows his mother is very lonely. He is her only son and wants to show respect to her and take care of her. After all, she gave much of her life to raise him. And he likes the idea of having family around. However, after living in the United States for more than three years, he has grown used to the American way of independence. He is also afraid his mother may not want to adjust to an American way of life so she might be very dependent on him. In addition he, and probably Hanna too, will be working all day so his mother would be alone for long hours. She, of course, would love to have grandchildren to take care of. In contrast, Hanna believes children come later. Hanna wants some time without kids or parents around to build a relationship with her husband. Hiro wants this, too, so he feels torn. He doesn't want to lose Hanna; however, he doesn't want to hurt his mother and destroy the loyalty he feels for her either. He feels "caught in the middle."

[5] *to let someone down:* to disappoint someone

**A. Discussion** Discuss these questions with your classmates.

1. What are two or three important things that Hiro should consider when thinking about what to do?

2. What should Hanna consider when thinking about what Hiro's mother wants?

**B.** In small groups, write in 3–4 sentences what you think Hiro should say to Hanna. Then write what you think he should say to his mother.

**To Hanna:**

_____

_____

_____

_____

**To his Mother:**

_____

_____

_____

_____

**C.** Using your sentences from B above, fill in the following two charts. In Chart 1, write reasons that Hiro might give Hanna for having his mother live with them and possible responses that Hanna might have. In the second chart, write reasons that Hiro might give his mother for not having her come to live with them now and possible responses that his mother might have (even though she may not say these things to him).

| Chart 1: Reasons Hiro Could Give Hanna | |
|---|---|
| Hiro's Reasons | Hanna's Responses |
| 1. My mother can cook for us when we are busy working. | 1. If she decides what we eat, she will want to make other decisions too. |
| 2. | 2. |
| 3. | 3. |
| 4. | 4. |

| Chart 2: Reasons Hiro Could Give His Mother | |
|---|---|
| Hiro's Reasons | Hiro's Mother's Responses |
| 1. It is too soon for you to live with us just after the wedding. Hanna and I need time to adjust to each other. | 1. But I want to be with my son and get to know Hanna, too. You are my family. |
| 2. | 2. |
| 3. | 3. |
| 4. | 4. |

**D.** Try to think of a possible solution that might be OK with Hiro's mother and with Hanna. Explain why your solution might work for each person.

## Vocabulary

ACTIVITY 3    **Academic Words** Write the letter of the correct definition in front of each word in the first column.

Words

1. _____ **intention**
2. _____ **restriction**
3. _____ **trapped**
4. _____ **interference**
5. _____ **permanently**
6. _____ **adjust**
7. _____ **relationship**
8. _____ **loyalty**
9. _____ **consideration**
10. _____ **independence**

Meanings

a. forever without change

b. freedom from control or influence

c. a limitation

d. make a change to fit in with something

e. in a situation with no way out

f. information to keep in mind when making a decision

g. a planned purpose

h. something which gets in the way of an action

i. commitment

j. the connection between two people or things

Fill each blank with one of the following nouns or verbs. Be sure to use the correct form.

income    appreciate    afford    contrast    adjust

When couples have too little (1) _____ to pay their bills and

(2) _____ the things they need, they may feel frustrated by the

(3) _____ between what they have and what they want to have. It helps

if they can (4) _____ their focus to what they have instead of what they

don't have. This way they (5) _____ more what they do have.

## Composition Analysis

**Conclusions in Essays**  The **conclusion** of an essay follows the body paragraphs; it is the very last part of the essay. Its most important function is to make the reader feel that the essay has come to completion. It should not leave the reader waiting for something more.

An effective conclusion begins with a well-focused introduction because the conclusion builds on the thesis statement to make a prediction, to offer a suggestion, to give an opinion, or simply to restate the thesis statement. Look at the following examples of different kinds of conclusion statements.

> **Prediction:** For the reasons presented here, couples need to gain independence by living separately from family members. Without this experience, they will never establish their own identity and never have the chance to be truly happy.

This is an effective conclusion because it first summarizes the main point of the essay. Then it makes a statement about what the author thinks will happen if couples do not follow the advice in the essay.

> **Suggestion:** Although living with family members can be difficult at times, it is important to consider the strengths of a family community in the home. Such a community offers many benefits.

This is an effective conclusion because it emphasizes the main point of the essay one more time. Then it encourages the reader to think positively about the idea of a family community.

> **Opinion:** Because of the many advantages of living with an extended family, families who live this way will be happier. They can enjoy the benefits of their own small community as well as avoid problems of isolation.

This is an effective conclusion because the writer sets up a cause and effect argument for his opinion. This logical support may help the reader accept the writer's point of view.

Look at the following statements. Put **E** in front of the ones that are effective conclusion statements. Then give reasons why you think they are effective. Put **NE** in front of the statements that are not effective. The first one is done for you.

1. ___E___ For several good reasons, adult children often find it difficult to keep their parents happy and have their own independence at the same time. However, it is essential for their happiness that they have their own lives.

   **Reason:** _This statement summarizes the reasons in the essay._

   _Then it gives an opinion._

2. _____ After considering both the advantages and disadvantages of using an Internet dating service, I think users must be extremely cautious because things can go terribly wrong.

   **Reason:** _____

   _____

3. _____ Despite the many similarities between British and American English, they differ in three important linguistic ways.

   **Reason:** _____

   _____

4. _____ Arranged marriages will never entirely replace love marriages because there will always be some people who want to follow their own hearts.

   **Reason:** _____

   _____

5. _____ As shown in this essay, if we do not pay attention to protecting our valuable forests, we may find that very soon we will have no forests to protect.

   **Reason:** _____

   _____

Now write a conclusion statement of your own and explain why it is effective.

6. _____

   _____

   **Reason:** _____

   _____

# *Writing 1*

**ACTIVITY 6**  To help you prepare for the writing assignment in Activity 7, choose a topic and discuss the questions with a partner who has chosen the same topic as you. Write answers to the questions in your own words. You do not need to agree with your partner as long as you can give reasons for your answers.

### Topic 1

1. What can Hiro do that Hanna might accept and that will still show respect for his mother?

2. How will this solution affect Hanna and his mother differently?

3. Why is this a good solution?

### Topic 2

1. Tell your partner about a difficult choice you have made in your life.

2. What were the feelings that pulled you in opposite directions?

**ACTIVITY 7**  **Writing Assignment**  Write an essay about one of the following topics. Be sure to include in your paper all of the items in the checklist on page 91.

### Topic 1

Write about a possible solution to Hiro's problem. Contrast the effects your solution will have on Hanna and Hiro's mother. Explain why you think your solution is a good one.

### Topic 2

Write about a decision in your life that was very difficult for you to make. Contrast the opposing feelings that you had. Tell what made you decide what to do in the end.

# Grammar

**Contrast Words and Phrases**

To show **contrast** between two ideas, a writer may use transition words and phrases. Look at the following sentence and notice how the word *while* sets up a contrast between two different beliefs.

> Some may believe in the benefits of an arranged marriage, **while** others have true faith only in a love marriage.

Writers use **subordinators, coordinators,** and **transition words and phrases** such as the ones in the following list to show contrast.

| Subordinators | Coordinators | Transition Words and Phrases |
|---|---|---|
| though | but | however |
| although | yet | on the one hand |
| even though | | on the other hand |
| while | | in contrast |
| | | conversely |

**ACTIVITY 8**    Find sentences from Reading 1 that provide examples of each of the three different kinds of contrast words above. Write them on the lines below. Underline the contrast word or phrase in each sentence.

1. **Subordinator:** _____

    _____

    _____

2. **Coordinator:** _____

    _____

    _____

3. **Transition Word or Phrase:** _____

    _____

    _____

Write your own sentence using a contrast word, then underline the word.

4. _____

    _____

    _____

Combine one sentence from Column A with another sentence from Column B and a **contrast word or phrase** from the list in the Grammar section to form a new sentence. Use a *different* contrast word or phrase for each combined sentence. Use correct punctuation. (See the Punctuation Summary in Appendix 4 on page 217.) The first one is done for you.

**Column A**

1. In the afternoon we ran around doing last minute shopping.
2. My sister likes coffee.
3. Hiro's mother wants her son to marry a girl she knows.
4. An arranged marriage is based on the choice of a third person.
5. I studied long hours.
6. Hanna wants to live only with Hiro.
7. Hiro's mother wants her son to live in Japan.
8. It is very expensive to travel to my home country.
9. My car needs new tires.

**Column B**

a. In the evening we stayed home and relaxed.
b. I very much want to visit my family.
c. Hiro wants to live with Hanna and his mother.
d. Hiro's mother doesn't know Hanna or her family.
e. I have no money to buy them.
f. I like tea.
g. Hiro wants to live in the United States.
h. I made time to be with my friends.
i. A love marriage is based on the love between two people.

1. *Although in the afternoon we ran around doing last minute shopping,*
   *in the evening we stayed home and relaxed.*

2. _____

   _____

3. _____

   _____

4. _____

   _____

5. _____

   _____

6. _____

   _____

7. _____

   _____

8. _____

   _____

9. _____

   _____

## Rewriting 1

ACTIVITY 10

**Peer Activity** Trade your paper from Activity 7 with another student. Read your partner's paper and see if the thesis statement provides a contrast. Then write the two things the writer contrasts at the top of the page. Next look at the conclusion and decide whether it makes a prediction, offers a suggestion, or gives an opinion. Talk to your partner about what you found and help him or her make any necessary changes.

ACTIVITY 11

**On Your Own** Review your partner's notes, your partner's comments, and your teacher's feedback on the first draft of your composition. Use the Composition Evaluation Sheet (from Appendix 1) that your teacher returned to you to see specifically what you need to improve. Then consider the questions in the checklist below. Finally, rewrite your paper to make it clearer and more meaningful.

✓CHECKLIST

**Content**

Does your thesis statement tell your point of view?

Do all of your points connect directly to the topic?

Does your conclusion include a prediction, a suggestion, or an opinion?

**Organization**

Does your thesis statement set up the contrast you will develop in your essay?

Do you develop your points through contrast?

Do your points follow a logical order?

Does your conclusion connect closely to your thesis statement?

**Grammar**

Do you use contrast and comparison words and phrases correctly?

## Reading 2: Extending the Topic Reading

This reading gives two very different personal opinions about marriage. One point of view favors arranged marriage while the other supports love marriage. Both have advantages.

As you read these two opinions, think about the advantages of each kind of marriage. You will use your thoughts later in this chapter.

## Arranged Marriage: Two Views

### View 1

1    It's no surprise to me that arranged marriages are not popular in the United States. Consider the great many freedoms that Americans have. They have freedom of speech, freedom of religion, and freedom of the press. In addition, they have the personal freedoms to choose where they go, where they live, and where they work. It only makes sense that Americans would also want to have the freedom to choose their own marriage partners. However, in the lifelong matter of marriage, I'm not so sure that freedom is the most important thing.

2    I come from Japan where we have two kinds of marriage: the so-called love marriage and the arranged marriage. We have more love marriages now than in the past, probably because of Western[6] influence, but up to half of all marriages are still arranged marriages. The arrangement begins when a young woman reaches marriageable age, now about 25 years of age. She and her parents put together a collection of information about her including family background, education, hobbies, accomplishments, interests, and a photo. Her parents then ask their

6 *Western:* referring to the United States and Canada

friends and acquaintances if any of them know a man who would make a good husband for their daughter. The person who does know such a man becomes the matchmaker and arranges a meeting if both the man and the woman are interested. This meeting will probably also include members from both families. If the meeting goes well, the couple will begin dating. The couple will usually receive advice and counsel from their parents and the matchmaker if they consider marriage, but the couple makes the final decision.

3    It is not uncommon for a woman to have several such introductions before she finds the man she wants to marry, so this kind of modern arranged marriage is not without some choice. I think this is a good method as long as no one puts pressure on the couple to choose marriage to each other. It is better for people who know the couple well to make introductions because love is unreliable. The person we love is not necessarily a person who will give us a good life, and when we are in love, often we can't see that. I know this is true because, in my country, the divorce rate for arranged marriages is lower than for love marriages.

4    Just as I get the advice and help of a professional if I want to buy a house, I want help in choosing a spouse because there will always be things I don't see myself. And a marriage partner is much more important than a house.

## View 2

5    I believe in freedom of speech, freedom of religion, freedom of the press, and freedom to do what I want with my own life. That's why I like living in America. I have the freedom to succeed and the freedom to fail, but either way, I am responsible. Therefore, I don't want anyone else to take any of the responsibility for that most personal of all decisions—who I marry.

6    It's unthinkable to me that anyone should try to influence me in a matter of my own heart. How can anyone but myself understand what will make me feel trust, genuine concern, love, and a shared sense of values? Furthermore, if I place someone else's advice above my own desires, won't I always wonder, "What if ... ? What if I had listened to my own feelings? What if I had chosen my own spouse from among those whom I most admire? Wouldn't I be happier and more satisfied?"

7    Besides, how can I be sure that if others advise me, they are not giving me opinions based on their own reasons rather than mine? For example, they may think that someone else will benefit from merging the two families. If that's what they think, how can they advise me honestly?

8    No, if I believe in myself and have the respect for myself that I deserve, I do not want an arranged marriage or even arranged dating. I must listen to my own heart. Then if I want someone else's advice, I will ask for it and afterwards decide if I want to take it or not. Consequently, if I make a mistake and get hurt, I have only myself to blame.

9    I want a marriage based on a love that my partner and I have created together before we decide to marry. I do not want a marriage based on what someone else thinks is best for me.

**Discussion** Discuss these questions with your classmates. You may wish to take some notes to use later in Activity 21.

1. What are the main differences between an arranged marriage and a love marriage?

2. Which do you prefer? Why?

3. Would you want to arrange a marriage for a son or daughter of yours? Why or why not?

4. What are some good points about an arranged marriage? What are some bad points?

5. What are some good points about a love marriage? What are some bad points?

**Group Activity** Reading 2 is about two contrasting views about marriage. In order to contrast two things, you must apply the same **point of comparison** to each. For example, if you are in the market to buy a car, you might use gas mileage as one point of comparison:

| Point of Comparison | Car A | Car B |
|---|---|---|
| Gas mileage | gets an average of 25 miles per gallon | gets an average of 31 miles per gallon |

Note that it is not meaningful to use two *different* points of comparison:

| Points of Comparison | Car A | Car B |
|---|---|---|
| Gas mileage and trunk space | gets an average of 25 miles per gallon | has more trunk space |

For each of the points of comparison in the chart below, fill in the columns to contrast arranged marriage and love marriage. Work in groups of 3–4 and share your answers with another group when you are finished.

| Points of Comparison | Arranged Marriage | Love Marriage |
|---|---|---|
| 1. Collection of information about possible marriage partners | part of marriage process | not part of marriage process |
| 2. Use of arranged first meeting of partners | meeting with a matchmaker and family members on both sides | |
| 3. Advice and counsel for marriage partners | | usually not part of marriage process |
| 4. Acceptance of reliability of love in the choice of a marriage partner | not accepted | |
| 5. Divorce rate | | |
| 6. Responsibility for choice of marriage partner | | completely with the couple |

# Vocabulary

ACTIVITY 14 **Academic Words**  Complete each statement below with a word from the following list. Be sure to use the correct form of the word. There may be more than one correct answer. You may use some words more than once and other words not at all.

| Words | Meanings |
|---|---|
| **accomplishment** | a success that has come through effort and hard work |
| **acquaintance** | a person who is not as close as a friend |
| **benefit** | to be helpful or useful |
| **collection** | a group of objects that have something in common |
| **create** | to bring into existence |
| **counsel** | the act of exchanging ideas, opinions, or advice |
| **hobby** | an activity done just for pleasure |
| **merging** | a coming together |
| **method** | a way of doing something |
| **professional** | a person who uses specialized training and knowledge to earn a living |
| **spouse** | a marriage partner |
| **unreliable** | not able to be counted on |

1. If you can make your play part of your work, then you are _____ your interests.

2. If your parents are planning an arranged marriage for you, they will give you _____ on who you should marry.

3. Usually many people _____ from a good marriage.

4. People are closer to their friends than to their _____.

5. _____ is an adjective you could use to describe a car that often breaks down.

6. Because of his many _____ he had not yet had time to find a wife.

7. It is both easier and costlier to hire a _____ to plan a wedding.

8. A good _____ to follow when accomplishing a goal is to make a plan and follow it through to the end.

9. Those who work hard can _____ great success.

10. My _____ and I have been together for twenty years, but still we are very different.

ACTIVITY 15 Fill in the missing word forms in the chart below. Use your dictionary to check word forms you don't know. An X means there is no common word form for a certain part of speech. (See Word Form Suffixes in Appendix 5 on page 219.)

| Noun (Thing) | Verb | Adjective | Adverb |
|---|---|---|---|
| | advise | | |
| | | | admirably |
| influence | | | |
| | marry | | X |
| | accomplish | | X |
| | | arranged | X |
| | | responsible | |
| unreliability | X | | |

# Composition Analysis

**Contrast and Comparison**  Although it is possible to compare and contrast in the same essay, it is simpler to do one or the other, not both. In the Grammar section on page 89, you learned about contrast statements used in the reading. You also practiced writing contrast statements.

When making a comparison, we use comparison words as follows:

Comparison Words

| Subordinators | Coordinators | Transition Words and Phrases | Key Words |
|---|---|---|---|
| just as | and | likewise | like |
| | and so | similarly | similar to |
| | also | in the same way | just like |
| | | | (be) similar to |
| | | | (be) the same as |

**Subordinator:**  **Just as** a boat floats on water, a ship floats too.
**Coordinator:**  A boat carries people or cargo across water **and so** does a ship.
**Transition Word:**  A boat works **in the same way** as a ship.
**Key Word:**  A boat **is similar to** a ship.

Use contrast words from the list below to make statements from the information you wrote in the chart in Activity 13. You may wish to go back and look at the work you did in Activities 8 and 9 before you do this activity. Use correct punctuation. (See the Punctuation Summary in Appendix 4 on page 217.)

For example,

| Points of Comparison | Arranged Marriage | Love Marriage |
|---|---|---|
| 1. Collection of information about possible marriage partners | Part of marriage process | Not part of marriage process |

*Although a collection of information about possible marriage partners is part of the arranged marriage process, it is not part of the love marriage process.*

| Contrast Subordinators | Contrast Coordinators | Contrast Transition Words and Phrases |
|---|---|---|
| though | but | however |
| although | yet | on the one hand |
| even though | | on the other hand |
| while | | in contrast |
| | | conversely |

1. _____

_____

2. _____

_____

3. _____

_____

4. _____

_____

5. _____

_____

6. _____

_____

Connect the following pairs of sentences using the **comparison words** on page 97. Use correct punctuation. (See the Punctuation Summary in Appendix 4 on page 217.) The first one is done for you.

1. Parents want what's best for their children. Adult children want their parents to be happy too.

   **in the same way:** _Parents want what's best for their children. In the_ _same way, adult children want their parents to be happy too._

2. I usually read very quickly when I read a newspaper. I often hurry when reading a magazine too.

   **just as** _____

   _____

3. My math teacher gives us a lot of homework. My English teacher makes us do a lot of homework.

   **and so** _____

   _____

4. I like to take my time when visiting an art museum. My best friend can spend hours looking at an art exhibit.

   **similarly** _____

   _____

5. My car is a little blue Toyota Corolla. My brother has a small blue Honda Civic.

   **is similar to** _____

   _____

6. I believe in love marriage. My boyfriend does not want an arranged marriage.

   **likewise** _____

   _____

# Making Connections

Choose main ideas from Reading 2 and find specific details in Reading 1 that support these main ideas.

| Main Idea from Reading 2 | Supporting Detail from Reading 1 |
|---|---|
| 1. *Young people need help with choosing a marriage partner.* | 1. *Hiro's mother would prefer that he marry a girl that she knows.* |
| 2. | 2. |
| 3. | 3. |
| 4. | 4. |

## American Weddings: A Reflection of American Values

1    Because the United States has historically been populated by immigrants from many lands, its marriage traditions come from a wide range of cultures. Perhaps this is why Americans are quite comfortable with a great diversity of rituals[7] and ceremonies. However, there are a few basic concepts that almost all U.S. weddings have in common which reflect some important American values. These often contrast with the values of other cultures.

2    First, in the United States, parental blessing is no more than a formality, rather than a necessity. Often a blessing will be requested as a courtesy to the parents. Often a couple will choose not to ask for a blessing at all. The union is more about the individuals than the families. This attitude reflects the American values of personal freedom, independence, and the equality of sons and daughters with their parents. While a young man and a young woman hope that both sets of parents will give their blessing to a union, the couple places higher importance on their own desires.

3    In contrast, in Sudan, for example, the bride and groom kiss the knees of their parents, a ceremony called *sungkem*, asking for forgiveness and blessing and promising to continue to serve their parents. This wedding ritual is held in front of a gargoyle[8] fountain. Water flowing from the gargoyle suggests the continuous flow of priceless parental love for their children. The ritual illustrates the position of honor, high status, and respect that children have for their parents.

4    Second, American marriages are not "arranged." A typical U.S. wedding takes place between two people who have looked for a partner themselves and have found someone they believe they can share their lives with. In other words, in the United States, where freedom and personal choice rule, marriages are based on love. They are not arranged to strengthen family business, influence, or position. Most of all, individuals do not give up their freedom of choice to any third person.

5    Conversely, in India, children are the property of their families until they are married. In addition, Indian parents have a strong sense of duty. They feel they are responsible for providing their children's marriage as well as their education. Therefore there is little tolerance for the American idea of freedom of choice in a marriage partner. The attitude held by millions of Indian women and men is that arranged marriage is the only choice. It is about the union of two families of similar background, in a community, in a caste,[9] in a religion, in a province, and in a country. It is what defines India's society, where ninety-five percent of marriages are arranged, even among people in the educated middle class.

6    Third, U.S. wedding ceremonies and wedding customs are among the most flexible in all the world. Whatever a person's ideas are about the perfect wedding, they will fit into the ideal of the American wedding tradition. There are no strict rules to follow. A wedding can be religious or civil. It can be formal or informal.

---

[7] *ritual:* a ceremonial act
[8] *gargoyle:* a strange imaginary creature, sometimes part human, part animal
[9] *caste:* social class based on family position

It can be large or small. It can follow or not follow the tradition that the bride wears white and the groom wears black. This reflects the American "live and let live"[10] attitude.

7    On the other hand, a traditional Pakistani wedding ritual is very formal and lasts four days. On the first day, the bride's and groom's families both dress in yellow. On the second day, the bride receives a traditional henna[11] staining of her hands and feet with beautiful symbolic patterns. Also, her family strings hundreds of colored lights around their home. On the day of the ceremony, the bride wears elaborate jewelry, a wedding gown, and a red veil while the groom wears a distinctive traditional turban. On the fourth day, the couple hosts their first dinner as husband and wife at the home of the groom's family. In such a society, the preservation of ritual and tradition are as important as freedom, personal choice, and flexibility are in the United States.

10    In conclusion, attitudes about marriage in the United States reflect the cultural values of freedom, independence, informality, flexibility, and defining one's own future. Other societies, however, have marriage conventions that reflect contrasting values. These include the preservation of long-standing ceremonial traditions as well as placing a higher value on family responsibility and structure than on individual freedom.

10 *live and let live:* show tolerance for others as you expect them to show tolerance for you
11 *henna:* a red dye made from the leaves of the henna plant

# Composition Analysis

**A Comparison/Contrast Essay**  The purpose of a **comparison/contrast essay** is to show how one thing is similar to or different from another. To do this, a writer will choose one or more points of comparison, then compare the two things, then draw a conclusion from the comparison.

**Point of Comparison:** _gas mileage_

**Comparison:** _Car A gets 25 miles per gallon of gas. Car B gets 30 miles per gallon._

**Conclusion:** _Car B is more fuel efficient than Car A._

**ACTIVITY 19**   In a group of 3–4, complete the following chart to compare American marriages and the marriages in some other cultures.

| Point of Comparison | American Marriages | Other Marriages | Conclusion |
|---|---|---|---|
| Attitudes about parents' blessing | Blessing is good but not essential | | Americans feel individual choice is more important than the respect for parents in Sudan. |
| Attitudes about tradition | | Tradition is important | |
| Attitudes about choice of marriage partner | | | |

# Writing 2

To help you prepare for the writing assignment in Activity 21, choose a topic and discuss the questions with a partner who has chosen the same topic as you. Write answers to the questions in your own words. You do not need to agree with your partner as long as you can give reasons for your answers.

### Topic 1

1. Do you feel that a marriage partner is a very personal choice between two people or can family or friends offer help?

2. Is love the most important part of marriage?

3. Do your feelings differ in any way from View 2 in Reading 2?

### Topic 2

1. What are some examples of responsibilities that adult children have to their parents in an extended family society?

2. What are some examples of responsibilities that parents have to their adult children?

3. How are these responsibilities different from those in a nuclear family?

### Topic 3

1. How do your ideas about marriage compare with American ideas?

2. Do you think American ideas about marriage represent American values?

3. What values do you think your ideas represent?

**ACTIVITY 21**  **Writing Assignment** Write a comparison/contrast essay about one of the following topics. Be sure to include in your paper all of the items in the checklist on page 108. You may wish to think back to some of your answers in Activity 12 to give you ideas.

### Topic 1

Compare your feelings about love marriage with View 2 of arranged marriage in Reading 2.

### Topic 2

Based on what you have learned in this chapter, contrast a society that is based on the extended family, such as Japan or India, with a society based on the nuclear family, such as the United States.

### Topic 3

Compare or contrast your own ideas about marriage with American attitudes toward marriage and the values they represent. Use examples from Reading 3 to support your points. You may wish to refer back to the chart you created in Activity 19.

**Factual Conditional Sentences**

Look at the following **factual conditional sentences** from Reading 2.

> The person who does know such a man becomes the matchmaker, and arranges a meeting if both the man and the woman are interested.

> If the meeting goes well, the couple will begin dating.

> No, if I believe in myself and have the respect for myself that I deserve, I do not want an arranged marriage or even arranged dating.

All of the sentences above have two clauses. One clause begins with *if*. This clause describes a "condition" or a special situation. Sometimes this clause is called the "*if*-clause." The second clause in the sentence shows a result. This clause describes what happens if the first clause is true. This kind of sentence is called a **factual conditional sentence**.

> Just as I get the advice and help of a professional if I want to buy a house, I want help in choosing a spouse because there will always be things I don't see myself.

"If I want to buy a house" is the condition and "I get the advice and help of a professional" is the result.

> Then if I want someone else's advice, I will ask for it …

The condition is "if I want someone else's advice" and the result is "I will ask for it."

**Factual conditional sentences** can occur in different tenses. These sentences use the present tense for the *if*-clause, and use the present or the future tense for the result clause. A conditional sentence can begin with the *if*-clause or the result clause.

**Present tense for the result clause**
If I make a mistake and get hurt, I have only myself to blame.

"If I make a mistake" is the condition and "I have only myself to blame" is the result clause. In this sentence the *if*-clause and a comma precede the result clause.

**Future tense for the result clause**
The couple will usually receive advice and counsel from their parents and the matchmaker if they consider marriage …

"The couple will usually receive advice and counsel from their parents and the matchmaker" is the result clause and "if they consider marriage" is the condition. In this sentence the result clause precedes the *if*-clause.

Combine each pair of sentences to write *one* **factual conditional sentence.** (There are two possibilities for each pair.) Be sure to use correct punctuation. Use pronouns when possible. The first one is done for you and shows both possible answers.

1. I ask my friends for advice.

   My friends give me advice.

   *If I ask my friends for advice, they give it to me.*

   or

   *My friends give me advice if I ask them for it.*

2. A couple wants to marry.

   A couple receives advice from family and the matchmaker.

   _____

   _____

3. I get the advice of a professional.

   I want to buy a house.

   _____

   _____

4. You believe that marriage is a matter of the heart.

   You will not be satisfied with an arranged marriage.

   _____

   _____

5. My family has their own reasons for wanting me to marry someone.

   How can I trust my family's advice?

   _____

   _____

6. I believe in myself.

   I can make my own decisions about who I marry.

   _____

   _____

7. Two people are in love and want to marry.

   Two people should be able to marry.

   _____

   _____

8. I want help.

   I will ask for help.

   _____

   _____

9. A person is very much in love.

   A person may not see that the one she loves will not provide a good life.

   _____

   _____

**ACTIVITY 23**   In front of each condition, write the letter of the appropriate result.

Condition

1. _____ If you want an American wedding,

2. _____ Some people say if you have enough love in your marriage,

3. _____ Other people say if you don't have more than love,

4. _____ If you are the son or daughter of Indian parents,

5. _____ If family responsibility is important to a couple,

6. _____ Some cultures feel that if love marriage is so wonderful,

7. _____ If you follow tradition in Sudan,

8. _____ If a love marriage is about the freedom to choose,

Result

a. your marriage will work.

b. you have great flexibility in the traditions you choose.

c. they may think less about their own desires.

d. why are there so many divorces?

e. you will kiss the knees of your parents on your wedding day.

f. your marriage will never work.

g. you are their property until you are married.

h. an arranged marriage is about responsibility to the chosen one.

# Rewriting 2

ACTIVITY 24 **Peer Activity**  Trade your paper from Activity 21 with another student. Read your partner's paper and underline the thesis statement. Find the two points that your partner compared or contrasted. Finally, check to see if the conclusion connects with the thesis statement. Then talk to your partner about what you found and help him or her make any necessary changes.

ACTIVITY 25 **On Your Own**  Review your partner's notes, your partner's comments, and your teacher's feedback on the first draft of your composition. Use the Composition Evaluation Sheet (from Appendix 1) that your teacher returned to you to see specifically what you need to improve. Then consider the questions in the checklist below. Finally, rewrite your paper to make it clearer and more meaningful.

> **✓ CHECKLIST**
>
> **Content**
> For Topic 1: Does your thesis statement set up the comparison you will develop in your essay?
> For Topic 2: Does your thesis statement set up the contrast you will develop in your essay?
> For Topic 3: Does your thesis statement set up the comparison or contrast you will develop in your essay?
> Does your conclusion include a prediction, a suggestion, or an opinion?
>
> **Organization**
> Do you develop your points through comparison or contrast?
> Do your details support your comparison or contrast?
> Does your conclusion connect closely to your thesis statement?
>
> **Grammar**
> Do you use contrast and comparison words correctly?
> Do you use factual conditional sentences correctly?

## Internet Activities

For additional activities related to this chapter, go to elt.thomson.com/catalyst.

# CHAPTER

# 5   Stereotypes and the Stereotyped

## Exploring the Topic

### ACTIVITY 1

**Discussion** The problem of stereotyping occurs when a person or group places a label on another person or group based only on appearance or insignificant information. Perhaps it is the natural reaction to making sense out of what is not understood. Perhaps it satisfies the immediate desire to separate oneself from what seems strange. Regardless of the cause, people suffer because stereotyping prevents communication. Once communication begins, stereotypes start to melt away.

In groups of 3–4, discuss the following questions. Then share your ideas with the class.

1. Do you think all people hold some kind of stereotypes? Explain.

2. What do you think people can do to avoid forming stereotypes?

3. How can people change their existing stereotypes?

4. What can you do to help other people change their stereotypes?

109

## PART 1

## *Reading 1:* Personal Experience Reading

This is a story about the experiences of a young Asian American girl growing up in New Jersey. As the events of her life show us, she is deeply affected by her association in people's minds with China, a place she has never been. China, it seems, plays a far greater role in her life than her home, New Jersey.

**As you read the story, think about the times that people respond to Helen as "a Chinese" instead of as "Helen Zia." You will use your thoughts later in this chapter.**

## Growing Up Asian American

1    There is a conversation that nearly all Asians in America have experienced more times than they can count. Total strangers, although well meaning, will interrupt to ask, "What are you?" or "Where are you from?" in the same way that they might ask about the breed of a dog. My standard reply to "What are you?" is "American," and to "Where are you from?" is "New Jersey." These, in my experience, cause great confusion. Eyebrows arch as the questioner tries again: "No, where are you really from?" I patiently explain that, really, I am from New Jersey. This always leads to something like, "Well then, what country are your people from?" Sooner or later I give in and tell them that my "people" are from China. But when I in turn ask, "And what country are your people from?" the reply is always a slightly annoyed, "I'm from America, of course."

2    Had I known more about my Asian American history I might have felt less foreign. Instead, I grew up thinking that perhaps China, a place I had never seen, was my true home, since so many people didn't think I belonged in America. I did

figure out, however, that relations between America and any Asian nation had a direct effect on me. Whenever a movie about Japan and World War II played at the local theater, my brothers and I became the enemy. It didn't matter that we weren't Japanese—we looked Japanese. My brothers and I would sit in the theater with all the other kids in town watching the brave Zero pilots[1] prepare an attack only to be intercepted by the all-American heroes—who were, of course, always white. Then the entire audience would scream, "Kill them, kill them, kill them!"—meaning the Japanese. When the movie was over and the lights came on, I wanted to be invisible so that my neighbors wouldn't think of me as an enemy.

3    Following World War II, it was China that was becoming the evil Communist threat. As a result, the FBI switched its attention from Japanese Americans to hundreds of Chinese Americans. My father was one. Consequently, our mail frequently arrived opened and damaged, and our phone reception[2] was sometimes poor. I thought everyone's mail service and phone lines were bad. Polite FBI agents interviewed our neighbors, asking if my father was up to anything unusual. Neighbor kids would come around and ask, "So what does your father do?" However, besides the suspicion of our neighbors, nothing ever came of the FBI investigations of my father, nor was a ring of Chinese American spies[3] ever found. Events like these did, however, succeed in creating a distrust of politics among the members of the Chinese American communities of the 1950s.

4    Like so many Asian immigrants, my father was unable to break into the American labor market and get a job so he was self-employed. His business of making "baby novelties" with little baby toys and pink or blue vases that he sold to flower shops became our business. Every day, in addition to doing our schoolwork, we helped out in the family business.

5    Our home was our workplace, the means to our livelihood, and therefore the center of everything—with our father in charge of it all. It was understood in our household that no one should ever disobey or argue with the father, who, in the Confucian[4] way, is God on earth. My mother, and of course the children, were expected to obey God absolutely. Growing up female, I could see the Confucian order in action: the daughter obeys the father, the wife obeys the husband, and, eventually, the widow obeys the son. The Confucian tradition was clearly not in my favor, as a girl.

6    I found similar lessons in the world beyond our walls. My Auntie Ching and her husband opened a Chinese restaurant at a major intersection of the highway. After they had spent their own money to upgrade the kitchen and remodel the restaurant, business was booming. However, Auntie Ching had no lease for the restaurant and the German American owner evicted the Chings to set up his own shop. Our tiny Chinese American community was horrified that the Chings would be treated so unfairly. My father urged them to fight it out in court. But they chose not to. Chinese cannot win, they said, so why make trouble for ourselves?

7    Similarly, when my parents were denied the right to rent or buy a home in various Philadelphia neighborhoods, they had to walk away even though my father was outraged. Moreover, we could only suffer in silence when my mother and her

---

[1] *Zero pilots:* Japanese pilots who flew the Zero Fighter planes in World War II

[2] *reception:* the quality of an electronic signal

[3] *spy:* a person employed to get secret information about an enemy

[4] *Confucian:* relating to the teachings of Confucius

troop of small children were thrown out of supermarkets because we were wrongly accused of opening packages and stealing. Or when my brother Henry was the only one of a group of noisy third graders who was expelled from the lunchroom for the rest of the year for talking. Or when my younger brother Hoyt and the few other Asian boys in school were rounded up because another kid said he thought he saw an "Oriental"[5] boy go into his locker. As a child, I just didn't see Chinese or other Asian Americans speaking up to question such injustices.

8    So, uncertain of my place in American society, I followed the Asian American behavior that I saw around me—silence and invisibility. I enjoyed school and, following my father's example, studied hard and performed well, but I avoided bringing attention to myself and rarely spoke up, even on matters related to me.

Excerpt from the book, *Asian American Dreams: The Emergence of an American People*, by Helen Zia.

[5] *Oriental:* of Asian background

ACTIVITY 2     **Discussion**  Discuss these questions with your classmates.

1. Was Helen Zia born in China or in America? Why is this important to her story?

2. In her first paragraph, Zia talks about how she answers the question, "Where are you from?" Why do you think she deals with the question in this way? What is her purpose?

3. Are there questions that people ask you about people from your birth country that bother you? How do you deal with these questions?

4. What do you think of her conclusion that the way to deal with unfair stereotyping is to remain silent and invisible? Is this what you do? Why or why not?

5. Give some examples of stereotypes that people have about the people of your ethnic background. How do these stereotypes make you feel?

## Vocabulary

ACTIVITY 3     **Academic Words**  Circle the letter of the definition that best matches the meaning of each **boldface** word.

1. Just as I was leaving work to go home, I was **intercepted** by my co-worker who wanted to tell me she needed my help.

    a. interrupted     b. insulted

2. If you don't pay your rent on time, your landlord might **evict** you.

    a. throw out     b. charge extra money

3. When the fog came across the road as I was driving, I was **horrified** at how little I could see.

    a. in the dark     b. shocked or unpleasantly surprised

4. If it rains where you have walked on a dirt road, your footsteps will be **invisible**.

    a. not able to be seen    b. muddy

5. I was **outraged** that my boss gave the promotion to someone else after I had worked so hard.

    a. extremely angry    b. extremely tired

6. After the accident, the police did an **investigation** to find out the cause.

    a. solution    b. detailed examination

7. A college or university can **expel** you if you copy material from a book and do not give credit to the author.

    a. refuse entrance    b. force someone to leave

8. One of the many **injustices** that immigrants face is job discrimination.

    a. unfair acts    b. difficult tasks

9. At the **intersection** of desire and opportunity is when great discoveries happen.

    a. meeting    b. passing

10. Often when immigrants come to the United States, they change their **livelihood** until they learn enough English to do their usual work.

    a. way of speaking at work    b. means of making a living

11. Most large American cities have many ethnic **communities** where English is rarely spoken.

    a. group of people with a common background or interest
    b. gathering places where people come to eat together

12. The U.S. has **labor** laws that do not allow children under 16 to work.

    a. having to do with work    b. having to do with creating jobs

**ACTIVITY 4**    In Reading 1, Helen Zia writes about many negative experiences she had when she was growing up as an Asian American. To help her describe these experiences she chooses words that have negative meanings.

Put a negative symbol (–) in front of the words below that you think have a negative meaning. Compare your answers with others and explain your answers.

| _____ horrified | _____ investigation | _____ suspicion |
|---|---|---|
| _____ denied | _____ interrupt | _____ intercepted |
| _____ labor | _____ accused | _____ annoyed |
| _____ invisible | _____ damaged | _____ expelled |
| _____ outraged | _____ threat | _____ evicted |
| _____ injustices | | |

# Composition Analysis

**Support for Opinions**  In Activity 4 you identified words that have a negative meaning. As Zia evaluates the effects of the stereotyping that surrounded her when she was growing up, the negative meaning of these words clearly affects the message that the reader receives. It supports the writer's opinion that negative situations existed which prevented her and other Asian Americans from living full and satisfying lives.

**ACTIVITY 5**   Identify the parts of Reading 1 which support the opinion that Asian Americans were prevented from living full and satisfying lives.

1. Because Reading 1 is an excerpt, not an essay, it does not have a thesis statement. What sentence in the second paragraph best tells what the excerpt is about?

   _____

   _____

2. What is the one word in this sentence that best expresses the writer's opinion? Does it have a positive or a negative meaning in the sentence?

   _____

   _____

3. What are the seven examples that the writer gives of situations that involve stereotyping of Asian Americans? Give a detail to support each example. The first one is done for you.

   a. **Example:** _At the movies I felt that my brothers and I became the_ _enemy because we look Japanese._

   **Supporting Detail:** _The audience would scream, "Kill them, kill them, kill them!"--meaning the Japanese. When the movie was over and the lights came on, I wanted to be invisible so that my neighbors wouldn't think of me as an enemy._

   b. **Example:** _____

   _____

   **Supporting Detail:** _____

   _____

c. Example: _____

_____

**Supporting Detail:** _____

_____

d. Example: _____

_____

**Supporting Detail:** _____

_____

e. Example: _____

_____

**Supporting Detail:** _____

_____

f. Example: _____

_____

**Supporting Detail:** _____

_____

g. Example: _____

_____

**Supporting Detail:** _____

_____

4. What does Zia conclude about the effects of Asian American stereotyping on her life?

_____

_____

**ACTIVITY 6**

To help you prepare for the writing assignment in Activity 7, choose a topic and discuss the questions with a partner who has chosen the same topic as you. Write answers to the questions in your own words. You do not need to agree with your partner as long as you can give reasons for your answers.

### Topic 1

1. What is one situation in Reading 1 in which Helen feels she is less than others because of some stereotype?

2. Why does she feel this way?

### Topic 2

1. Tell your partner about a situation in your life in which you felt less than others because of some stereotype.

2. Why did you feel this way?

**ACTIVITY 7**

**Writing Assignment** Write an essay about one of the following topics. Be sure to include in your paper all of the items in the checklist on page 119.

### Topic 1

The author of Reading 1 gives examples in paragraphs 1, 2, 3, 5, 6, and 7 of ways that she feels Asian Americans are prevented from living full and satisfying lives. Choose one of these examples, explain it, and write about how it supports this point of view.

### Topic 2

Choose a situation from your own life that gives an example of one way that you feel you have been prevented from living a full and satisfying life because of some stereotype. Write about how the situation supports your point of view.

# Grammar

**Run-on Sentences**

A **run-on sentence** is a compound sentence that is incorrectly punctuated. It is important to understand that it is the punctuation, not the length of the sentence, that makes it a run-on sentence.

*Incorrect:* Our home was our workplace our father was in charge of it all.

*Correct:* Our home was our workplace **and** our father was in charge of it all.

There are three common ways to fix run-on sentences:

1. Separate the two independent clauses with a period to make two sentences.

   *Incorrect:* Helen's father was unable to break into the American labor market his business was selling "baby novelties."

   *Correct:* Helen's father was unable to break into the American labor market. His business was selling "baby novelties."

2. Use a semicolon, not a comma, between two independent clauses.

   *Incorrect:* The lights came on after the movie Helen wanted to be invisible.

   *Correct:* The lights came on after the movie; Helen wanted to be invisible.

3. Put a coordinating conjunction, such as **and, but, or, for, yet, nor,** or **so,** after the comma between two independent clauses.

   *Incorrect:* We were very tired by the end of our project, we completed it on time.

   *Correct:* We were very tired by the end of our project, but we completed it on time.

4. Use a subordinating conjunction, such as **after, although, before, unless, as, because, even though, if, since, until, when,** or **while,** before one of two independent clauses.

   *Incorrect:* Helen was an Asian American, many people thought she was Chinese.

   *Correct:* Although Helen was an Asian American, many people thought she was Chinese.

5. Replace the comma between two independent clauses with a semicolon and transitional word, such as **however, moreover, on the other hand, nevertheless, instead, also, therefore, consequently, otherwise,** or **as a result.** Place a comma after the transition word.

   *Incorrect:* Helen's father urged the Chings to go to court, they would not.

   *Correct:* Helen's father urged the Chings to go to court; however, they would not.

| ACTIVITY 8 | Rewrite the following paragraph, putting in punctuation and adding subordinators and coordinators to correct the run-on sentences. Delete words only if they do not affect the meaning and it is necessary for correct grammar. |
|---|---|

Helen Zia felt misunderstood by people around her she felt that people thought of her as Chinese she had never even seen China she felt American she and her family suffered some very unfair stereotyping she was unsure of her role in the American society around her she followed her father's example and became successful in school she also learned to avoid bringing attention to herself and to refrain from speaking up by watching other Asian Americans around her.

_____

_____

_____

_____

_____

| ACTIVITY 9 | Decide if each of the following sentences is correct or incorrect. If it is correct, write C in the blank. If it is incorrect, write IC and correct it. Be sure you do not change the meaning. |
|---|---|

_____ 1. Can't you stop that it's driving me crazy?

_____ 2. Hurry. We're going to be late.

_____ 3. Stereotypes are so destructive. Because they cut off communication.

_____ 4. There is a stereotype. That anyone who looks Chinese is not really American.

_____ 5. The library closes at 9 PM and it's 8:40 now so if we don't leave right away we won't have the book we need to complete our report by tomorrow.

_____ 6. When people have too little knowledge of individuals, they form stereotypes about people they see as different.

_____ 7. The meeting is tomorrow morning make sure you bring your laptop for the presentation.

_____ 8. Anwar returned with the missing documents we knew that everything was going to be OK.

# Rewriting 1

**ACTIVITY 10**

**Peer Activity** Trade your paper from Activity 7 with another student. Read your partner's paper. Identify the situation involving stereotyping that the essay is about. Then identify the thesis statement and make sure the controlling idea gives a point of view about the situation. Does the essay support this point of view with examples? Talk to your partner about what you found and help him or her make any necessary changes.

**ACTIVITY 11**

**On Your Own** Review your partner's notes, your partner's comments, and your teacher's feedback on the first draft of your composition. Use the Composition Evaluation Sheet (from Appendix 1) that your teacher returned to you to see specifically what you need to improve. Then consider the questions in the checklist below. Finally, rewrite your paper to make it clearer and more meaningful.

---

**✓CHECKLIST**

**Content**

Does your thesis statement give your point of view about the situation?

Does your essay stick to the focus of the topic?

Do you give adequate support for your point of view through examples and explanation?

**Organization**

Does your thesis statement identify what stereotyping example you are writing about?

Do the positive or negative meanings of your words fit with your point of view?

Does your conclusion successfully mark the end of your essay by connecting to your thesis statement and making an interesting point?

**Grammar**

Do you avoid run-on sentences?

---

## PART 2

# Reading 2: Extending the Topic Reading

This reading shows how labels learned at a young age can lead to harmful racist stereotyping. The use of food names to describe people's behavior is one way that racist attitudes find their way into everyday life.

As you read the story, think about how labels changed the thinking and behavior of Jeanne Park, the writer. You will use your thoughts later in this chapter.

## Eggs, Twinkies, and Ethnic Stereotypes

1    Who am I?

2    For Asian American students, the answer is a serious, hardworking, and intelligent young person. However, living up to[6] this reputation has secretly been very hard for me.

3    The expectations begin in elementary school. It's not uncommon for a teacher to remark, "You're Asian; you're supposed to do well in math." The real message is, "You're Asian and you're supposed to be smarter."

4    This is not to say that being labeled intelligent isn't flattering, because it is. Nor can I say that being at the top of my class isn't ego-boosting, because it certainly is. However, at a certain point, the pressure became crushing. I felt as if doing poorly on my next spelling quiz would stain the reputation of all Asian students forever.

5    So I continued to be an academic overachiever, as were my friends. By junior high school I started to believe I really was smarter. I looked down on non-Asians. I was a bigot; all my friends were Asians. I really didn't think of mingling with anyone else.

6    My superior opinion of Asian students changed, however, in high school. As a student at one of the nation's most competitive science and math schools, I found that being on top was no longer easy. I quickly learned that Asian students are not smarter. How could I ever have believed such a thing? All around me were intelligent, hard working people who were not only Asian but white, black, and Hispanic.

7    Social segregation does still exist in the schools, however. With few exceptions, each race mixes only with its "own kind." Students see one another in the classroom, but outside the classroom there remains a clear separateness.

8    A whole racist vocabulary even exists. An Asian student who socializes only with other Asians is believed to be an Asian Supremacist, one who thinks Asians are better than other people. Yet an Asian student who socializes only with whites is called a "twinkie,"[7] one who is yellow on the outside but white on the inside. A white teenager who socializes only with whites is thought of as prejudiced. Yet one who socializes with Asians is considered an "egg," white on the outside and yellow on the inside.

---

[6] *to live up to*: to equal some expectation
[7] *Twinkie*: a sweet snack which has a yellow crust on the outside and white cream on the inside

9   These food names can go on endlessly, leaving many people confused, and leaving many more fearful of social interactions. Because these stereotypes are almost completely accepted, they are rarely questioned. Therefore many people develop harmful stereotypes of entire races. The truth is, we label people before we even know them. And, unfortunately, labels learned at a

**Twinkies®**

young age later grow into more serious acts of racism. For example, my parents once accused and then fired a Puerto Rican cashier because they believed she had stolen $200 from their grocery store. They later learned it was a mistake.

10   We all hold dangerous stereotypes of people that limit us because we cheat ourselves out of what different cultures can offer. We can grow and learn from each culture whether it be Chinese, Korean, or African American. Therefore, stereotyping hurts not just those who are stereotyped, but also those who do the stereotyping. In short, it hurts everyone. Just recently some Asian boys in my neighborhood were attacked by a group of young white boys who called themselves the Master Race. I don't feel angry about this act. Instead, I feel sorry for a generation that lives in a state of bigotry.

11   It may be too late for our parents' generation to accept that each person can only be judged as an individual. However, with effort and understanding, we can do better by refusing to accept stereotyping as a way of life.

---

**ACTIVITY 12**   **Discussion** Discuss these questions with your classmates.

1. What is the meaning of the title?

2. Why was Park, the writer, an overachiever in school?

3. Why does the author object to "food names"? How do they affect those who are given them?

4. Does the author believe that racism will improve? Give at least two details that support your answer.

5. How does Park answer the question, "Who am I?" How would you describe who she is?

**Group Activity** Your teacher will put you in groups of three or four students representing at least two different nationalities. In your group, go back to question 5 in Activity 2 on page 112. Discuss with your group stereotypes that exist in your home country and make a list of answers to questions 1–3 for each nationality represented in your group.

1. What groups of people are stereotyped in each of the cultures represented in your group?

2. What do people say about these groups of people?

3. How do people treat them?

Next consider all of the nationalities together.

4. Are there similarities in items 2 and 3 in the different cultures represented in your group? What are these similarities?

5. Why do you think these similarities exist?

Share your answers with another group or with your class.

## Vocabulary

ACTIVITY 14 **Academic Words** Choose the word that has a similar meaning as the **boldface** word or words.

1. In junior high school, Park **had the attitude that Asians were smarter and better than non-Asians.**

   a. was racist        b. was confused

2. The writer tells us that an Asian student who socializes only with whites is **given the name** "twinkie."

   a. accused        b. labeled

3. Beginning in elementary school, Park got good grades in her **school** subjects.

   a. academic        b. overachiever

4. **Separation of races** in a population occurs when the people hold stereotypes.

   a. segregation        b. mingling

5. Stereotypes could not exist if we all considered the value of **people one person at a time without connection to a group.**

   a. as individuals        b. as separate groups

6. The fruits and vegetables at the farmer's market are **of a higher quality** than those at the supermarket.

   a. crushing        b. superior

7. When your teacher **praises** you for an essay you wrote, you feel happy.

   a. accuses        b. flatters

8. When different races have **communication and work together**, they can better solve common problems.

  a. racism          b. interaction

9. Park was **smart** in school, but it was not until she was in high school that she realized that whites and blacks and Hispanics were smart too.

  a. intelligent      b. racist

10. I hope that **people of a similar age as me** can do better at refusing to accept stereotypes than our parents did.

  a. my reputation    b. my generation

## Composition Analysis

**Essay Titles**  An essay should have a **title**. The title introduces the main point of the essay and should not be too specific. It is usually a phrase, perhaps one from the essay, not a complete sentence. All of the content words in the title are capitalized. For example,

> **Eggs, Twinkies, and Ethnic Stereotypes**

Three strategies that writers use to create titles are the following:

1. **Using words that have a double meaning.** The title of Reading 3 below is "Model Minority." The word "model" in this title leads us to think that the minority in this essay enjoys a very positive status in the minds of the people around them. But, on the contrary, the essay tells us that in several ways Asian Americans are worse off than some other minorities and that this term "model minority" may actually work against them.

2. **Using interesting or unusual words that provide examples of the main point in order to catch the reader's curiosity.** In the title of Reading 2, "Eggs, Twinkies, and Ethnic Stereotypes," the writer uses the words "eggs" and "Twinkies" to represent stereotypes based on food vocabulary. The result is that the reader wonders what the connection is between these two kinds of food and racial stereotypes.

3. **Using a phrase that either comes directly from the thesis statement or restates generally the main idea in the thesis statement.** The title of Reading 3 in Chapter 3, "Breaking Barriers Through Athletics," is an example of this strategy. The title of Reading 3 in Chapter 2, "Prisoners Without Cause," is another example.

The title of Reading 1 is "Growing Up Asian American." Read this story again and consider the main idea. Decide which of the three strategies above you think applies to this title. Give a reason for your answer. Then try to think of your own title for Reading 1. What strategy did you use?

**Title strategy number for Reading 1:** _____

**Reason:** _____

**Your own title for Reading 1:** _____

**Strategy number:** _____

## Making Connections

Below is a list of ways that Zia in Reading 1, Park in Reading 2, or both Zia and Park have experienced the painful injustice of stereotyping. Write a **Z** if it is a pressure that Zia experienced, write **P** if it is a pressure that Park experienced, and write **ZP** if it is something they both experienced. Following each item, write the paragraph number from Reading 1 and/or Reading 2 where you found the information that supports your answer.

_____ 1. You must do well in school because it is expected of Asian Americans.

   Reading 1, paragraph _____    Reading 2, paragraph _____

_____ 2. You must not argue for your rights.

   Reading 1, paragraph _____    Reading 2, paragraph _____

_____ 3. People think of me as an enemy.

   Reading 1, paragraph _____    Reading 2, paragraph _____

_____ 4. Stereotypic attitudes can be slow to change.

   Reading 1, paragraph _____    Reading 2, paragraph _____

_____ 5. As an Asian American, you cannot live in certain neighborhoods.

   Reading 1, paragraph _____    Reading 2, paragraph _____

_____ 6. Asian kids get into trouble more than white kids.

   Reading 1, paragraph _____    Reading 2, paragraph _____

_____ 7. You must be hardworking because it is expected of Asian Americans.

   Reading 1, paragraph _____    Reading 2, paragraph _____

_____ 8. You must not speak up or draw attention to yourself if you are Asian American.

   Reading 1, paragraph _____    Reading 2, paragraph _____

_____ 9. There is a social separation between races.

Reading 1, paragraph _____      Reading 2, paragraph _____

_____ 10. Stereotypes can be very destructive to those who are stereotyped.

Reading 1, paragraph _____      Reading 2, paragraph _____

## Reading 3: Academic Reading

## Model Minority

1    The stereotypes of Asian Americans have changed greatly over the years. A century ago, Asian Americans were considered lazy and stupid. Since that time, the phrase "model minority" has been used to describe Asian Americans as a hard-working, well-educated, successful minority race. However, while the term "successful race" might seem positive at first, there are several reasons why the phrase "model minority" is rejected by many Asian Americans.

2    Despite the conclusions about Asian Americans based on the myth[8] of a model minority, the facts tell a different story. For instance, Asian Americans are twice as likely to be poor as non-Hispanic whites. Asian Americans also have an illiteracy[9] rate that is over five times that of non-Hispanic whites.

[8] _myth:_ an untruth or half-truth
[9] _illiteracy:_ the condition of being unable to read or write

3   But the myth of the model minority isn't entirely false. According to Census Bureau data, there is some truth to the idea that Asian Americans are better educated and more successful. For instance, over twenty-six percent of Asian Americans have at least a Bachelor's degree, compared with seventeen percent of all Americans. However, on the other hand, the numbers also show that Asian Americans fall into the lower end of the scale. In March of 1999, over eight percent of Asian Americans aged twenty-five and over had earned less than a ninth grade education, compared with seven percent of all Americans.

4   Research is also beginning to suggest that the pressures placed on Asian Americans due to the model minority stereotype may be the cause of feelings of isolation[10] and depression.[11] In fact, according to the American Psychological Association, Asian American women have the highest suicide[12] rate among all women aged 15–24. Also, Asian American boys in grades 5 through 12 reported physical abuse at twice the rate of white boys.

5   Andrew Chin and Judy Tseng have made an effort to inform, educate, and empower Asian Americans through a website called ModelMinority.com. They argue that the model minority stereotype negatively affects Asian Americans in two ways. First, the focus on Asian American success serves to hide the problems Asian Americans continue to face from racial discrimination in all areas of life. Second, by using Asian American success to prove that America rewards anyone who works hard, it excuses American society from addressing the issues of race in general, particularly racism against Asian Americans.

6   Although Asian Americans enjoy a more positive reputation than in the past, it has worked against them with policymakers[13] and the general population. Because people think of them as the "model minority," their needs in education, employment, and other areas are under-served. Not only does this cause Asian Americans to suffer, but it weakens the entire community.

10 *isolation:* separateness from others
11 *depression:* feelings of extreme sadness and helplessness
12 *suicide:* the act of killing oneself
13 *policymakers:* people who make the decisions about the actions of a government

## Composition Analysis

**An Argument Essay**  The writer's purpose in an **argument essay** is to persuade the reader of one way of looking at an issue. When writing this kind of essay, the writer may use description, narration, cause and effect, or comparison and contrast to present reasons for his or her point of view. The reasons will probably include some opinions supported by facts. The reader needs the opinion to understand the context of the facts. The reader needs the facts to decide whether the opinion seems convincing. For example,

**Opinion:** Many Chinese arrive in the United States without much education.

**Fact:** Nine percent of the Chinese who have arrived in New York City since 1990 do not have a high school degree.

Write the letter of the fact in the blank that supports each of the following opinions. There may be more than one correct answer.

Opinions

_____ 1. The pressures placed on Asian Americans due to the model minority stereotype may be the cause of feelings of isolation and depression.

_____ 2. The myth of the model minority contains some truth.

_____ 3. Despite the conclusions about Asian Americans based on the myth of a model minority, the facts tell a different story.

_____ 4. Asian Americans also fall into the lower end of the education scale.

_____ 5. Women have an especially hard time dealing with the model minority stereotype.

_____ 6. Not all Asian Americans are academic overachievers.

Facts

a. Asian American boys in grades 5 through 12 reported physical abuse at twice the rate of white boys.

b. Over eight percent of Asian Americans aged twenty-five and over had earned less than a ninth grade education, compared with seven percent of all Americans.

c. Asian Americans are twice as likely to be poor as non-Hispanic whites.

d. Over twenty-six percent of Asian Americans have at least a Bachelor's degree, compared with seventeen percent of all Americans.

e. Asian American women have the highest suicide rate among all women aged 15–24.

f. Asian Americans also have an illiteracy rate that is over five times that of non-Hispanic whites.

**Topic Sentences as Predictors** In Chapter 1, you learned how topic sentences predict the kind of information that you will find in a paragraph. Look at the following example from paragraph 8 of Reading 2:

> **Topic Sentence:** A whole racist vocabulary even exists.

> **Prediction:** The paragraph will give more details about racist vocabulary.

For the following paragraphs from Reading 3, write the topic sentence, then circle the letter of the correct prediction of what the paragraph will probably be about.

1. **Topic Sentence of Paragraph 1:** _____
   _____

   a. how the stereotypes Asian Americans have of others have changed

   b. how stereotypes of Asian Americans have changed

   c. how Asian Americans have changed

2. **Topic Sentence of Paragraph 2:** _____
   _____

   a. examples of how Asian Americans are the best model minority

   b. a comparison of Asian Americans to non-Hispanic whites

   c. examples of how Asian Americans are not completely a model minority

3. **Topic Sentence of Paragraph 3:** _____
   _____

   a. examples that show it is false that Asian Americans are a model minority

   b. examples that suggest that in some ways Asian Americans really are a model minority

   c. examples that suggest it is a myth that any group of people can be a model minority

4. **Topic Sentence of Paragraph 4:** _____
   _____

   a. examples that suggest the model minority stereotype is not good for Asian Americans

   b. how research is causing Asian Americans to have feelings of isolation and depression

   c. how pressure on Asian Americans is leading to new research

5. **Topic Sentence of Paragraph 5:** _____

_____

    a. ways that the model minority stereotype is affecting Asian Americans

    b. how a website called ModelMinority.com is helping Asian Americans

    c. how Andrew Chin and Judy Tseng put together their website

# Writing 2

**ACTIVITY 19**

To help you prepare for the writing assignment in Activity 20, choose a topic and discuss the questions with a partner who has chosen the same topic as you. Write answers to the questions in your own words. You do not need to agree with your partner as long as you can give reasons for your answers.

### Topic 1

1. In what way do food names have a bad effect on Park's life?

2. Tell your partner about a time when someone gave you a name you thought did not fit you.

3. How did you feel about this name?

### Topic 2

1. Why do some Asian Americans think the term "model minority" does them harm?

2. Tell your partner about a time when someone gave you a name that seemed positive but you thought it was negative.

**ACTIVITY 20**

**Writing Assignment** Write an **argument essay** on one of the following topics. Be sure to include in your paper all of the items in the checklist on page 132.

### Topic 1

Describe how Park's own experiences in Reading 2 support her point of view that food names are destructive and dangerous. Include one experience of your own when someone gave you a label you thought was unfair. Explain how you felt about it.

### Topic 2

Describe how the label "model minority" in Reading 3 supports the point of view that even a label that seems positive can be negative. Include one experience of your own when someone gave you a label that didn't seem negative, but it hurt you.

# Grammar

| The Present Perfect and Past Perfect Verb Tenses | The **present perfect** verb tense is used to express actions that happened at an indefinite time in the past. Writers use it when the exact time of the action is less important than the action itself. The present perfect is formed with **have** or **has** + the **past participle** of the main verb. |

The stereotypes of Asian Americans **have changed** greatly over the years.

In this sentence, the important point is that stereotypes of Asian Americans have changed, not when they changed.

There is a conversation that nearly all Asians in America **have experienced** more times than they can count.

In this sentence, the frequency of the experience is all that matters. When the experience occurred does not matter at all.

How could I ever **have believed** such a thing?

In this sentence, the focus is on surprise that a belief of the past has changed. Again, the time of the change is not important.

The **past perfect** verb tense is used to show that something happened before a specific time in the past. It always shows a relationship between two events. The past perfect is formed with **had** + the **past participle** of the main verb.

In March of 1999, over eight percent of Asian Americans aged twenty-five and over **had earned** less than a ninth grade education.

There are two times in this sentence—March of 1999 and the time when over eight percent of Asian Americans aged twenty-five or over got their less than ninth-grade education. The use of the past perfect lets us know that the education event came before March of 1999.

Instead, I grew up thinking that perhaps China, a place I **had** never **seen**, was my true home.

The time order in this sentence is that the writer had not been to China before the time when she thought that perhaps China was her true home.

**Had I known** more about my Asian American history, I might have felt less foreign.

In this sentence, knowing more about her Asian American history is the cause of the possible effect of her feeling less foreign. In real time, cause must precede effect.

---

**ACTIVITY 21** | Fill each blank with the correct form of the verb in parentheses. Use the present perfect or the past perfect.

1. Until high school, Park (believe) _____ that Asians really were smarter than non-Asians.

2. Park's superior opinion of Asian students (**change**) _____ by the time she got through high school.

3. Asian Americans (**be**) _____ a hard-working and dedicated people since they started coming to America in the 1860s, but public opinion _____ not always (**agree**) _____.

4. Americans (**consider**) _____ Asian Americans lazy and stupid before they called them the "model minority."

5. The successes of Asian Americans (**serve**) _____ to hide the problems of racial discrimination that Asian Americans face.

6. Although Asian Americans enjoy a more positive reputation than in the past, it (**work**) _____ against them with policymakers and the general population.

7. Research (**suggest**) _____ that feelings of isolation and depression among Asian Americans may be the result of the model minority stereotype.

8. Asian Americans (**have**) _____ to be strong to deal with the discrimination they (**suffer**) _____.

**ACTIVITY 22** | Find the eight present perfect or past perfect errors in the following paragraph and correct them.

Why do people form stereotypes? After all, we had learned that stereotypes are inaccurate at best and dangerous at worst. Could it be that we are lazy? If a person has offend me, it is easier for me to think badly of him than to learn about him as an individual. Could it be that we want to fit in with common ways of thinking? If I was followed the opinions of others then I have the comfort of a group, whereas if I have followed my own opinions I may have standed alone. Could it be that we sometimes want to have someone to blame our troubles on? If I have lost my job or I has been paid too little, it is easier to blame immigrants or some other group than to look to myself for a solution. Could it be that we stereotype for some or all of these reasons? It is safe to say that, unfortunately, we had all sometimes form stereotypes to meet our own needs.

## Rewriting 2

**ACTIVITY 23**  **Peer Activity** Trade your paper from Activity 20 with another student. Read your partner's paper. Check to see if the title suggests the beginning of an answer to the question in the topic. Then check to see if the thesis statement either gives an answer to the question or organizes how the question will be answered. Next, check that the topic sentences support the thesis statement and that clear, concrete details support the topic sentences. Can you find any run-on sentences? Then talk to your partner about what you found and help him or her make any necessary changes.

**ACTIVITY 24**  **On Your Own** Review your partner's notes, your partner's comments, and your teacher's feedback on the first draft of your composition. Use the Composition Evaluation Sheet (from Appendix 1) that your teacher returned to you to see specifically what you need to improve. Then consider the questions in the checklist below. Finally, rewrite your paper to make it clearer and more meaningful.

---

**✓ CHECKLIST**

**Content**

Do you have a title that fits your essay?

Do you have a thesis statement that addresses the question(s) in the topic?

Does your essay stick to the focus of the topic?

Do you give adequate support for your point of view through examples and explanation?

**Organization**

Do your paragraphs have clear topic sentences supported by relevant concrete details?

Does your conclusion include a prediction, a suggestion, or an opinion?

Do your points follow a logical order?

**Grammar**

Do you avoid any run-on sentences?

Do you use the present perfect and past perfect verb tenses correctly?

---

## Internet Activities

For additional activities related to this chapter, go to elt.thomson.com/catalyst.

## Exploring the Topic

**ACTIVITY 1**

**Discussion** Assimilation takes time. Some immigrants are eager to "Americanize" so it may go more quickly. Others may not want to assimilate for fear of losing their personal identity or because they do not feel a part of what they see in America. Still others may not think about assimilation at all until events occur that make them feel different.

In groups of 3–4, discuss the following ideas and questions. Then share your ideas with the class.

1. What new things were easy for you to adjust to when you came to the United States?

2. What new things do you feel you will never adjust to? Why?

3. Do you feel different when you do certain things such as socialize or eat?

4. Is it important for you to be a part of the culture around you or do you prefer to associate with people of your own culture? Or do you prefer to be by yourself? Explain.

## PART 1

## Reading 1: Personal Experience Reading

Maria Jacinto is one of many Mexican immigrants who lives among other Mexican immigrants and does not want to give up her Mexican identity. Moreover, she is not sure she wants her children to accept the American values of the "blondies." More than ever before, immigrants have the opportunity to assimilate as much or as little as they want to.

As you read this story, think about why the Jacintos have more assimilation choices than immigrants in the past. You will use your thoughts later in this chapter.

### Immigrants Resisting Idea of Assimilation

1    Night is falling on Omaha, Nebraska,[1] and Maria Jacinto is making tortillas for the evening meal. She lives in a small house with her husband and five children in a neighborhood where most of the residents are Mexican immigrants. Like their neighbors, the Jacintos mix the old country with the new one as they face some kind of assimilation.

2    Maria Jacinto, who speaks only Spanish, stresses a need to maintain the family's Mexican heritage.[2] At the same time, her 11-year-old bilingual[3] son comes in and joins his brothers and sisters in the living room to watch "The Simpsons." He is wearing a San Francisco 49ers jacket and has a paper route.[4]

[1] *Omaha, Nebraska:* a city and state in the central United States
[2] *heritage:* background
[3] *bilingual:* speaking two languages
[4] *paper route:* a job delivering newspapers

3    Jacinto became a U.S. citizen last April, but she does not feel like an American. In fact, she seems resistant to the idea of assimilating into U.S. society. "I think I'm still a Mexican," she says. "When my skin turns white and my hair turns blonde, then I'll be an American."

4    The experiences of the Jacinto family are in many ways typical of the slow process of assimilation that brings many immigrants into the American mainstream. That process is nothing new in Omaha, which drew Czechs, Germans, and Irish in great numbers in the early 1900s.

5    However, something very different is also happening in the middle of the great American "melting pot."[5] As immigrant populations reach large numbers in many communities, they are changing American society more than the melting pot is changing them. Of course American culture remains a powerful force—for better or worse. It influences people both here and around the world in countless ways. However, immigrants now have a choice. They can resist Americanization if they want to. There are several reasons why they may make this choice.

6    Never before have so many immigrants come from a single country—Mexico, from a single language base—Spanish, or from a country that borders the United States. Today Hispanics, mostly of Mexican origin, make up thirty-one percent of the population of California and twenty-eight percent of the population of Texas. Since 1970, more than half of the estimated twenty million foreign-born people who have settled in the United States (legally and illegally) have been Spanish speakers. This means that Mexican immigrants have the opportunity to develop much greater connection with each other than previous immigrant groups.

7    As a result, the idea of assimilation is coming into question. It no longer seems to mean following the ways of those who are native born. Also with today's emphasis on diversity, it has become easier than ever for immigrants to avoid the melting pot entirely. Terms such as "salad bowl" and "mosaic,"[6] which suggest a sense of separateness, are coming into favor. They are replacing the term "melting pot," which suggests a blending together.

8    Moreover, families such as the Jacintos constantly worry about the bad influences of assimilating with Americans. They see their children assimilating, but often to aspects of American culture they do not agree with. "It's difficult to adapt to the culture here," said Maria Jacinto, who moved to the United States ten years ago. "In the Hispanic tradition, the family comes first, not money. It's important for our children not to be influenced too much by the *gueros*," she said. This term means "blondies" but she uses it to describe Americans. "I don't want my children to be influenced by immoral[7] things." Over the loud noise of the television in the next room, she asked, "Not all families here are like the Simpsons, are they?"

9    Immigrants such as the Jacintos are here to stay but remain unsure of their new country.

---

[5] *melting pot:* the metaphor that refers to America as a country where immigrants blend together and all become part of one great substance like a soup

[6] *mosaic:* small pieces fitted together to make a whole

[7] *immoral:* not conforming to standards of acceptable behavior

**Discussion** Discuss these questions with your classmates.

1. Why is Maria Jacinto not sure she wants to be an American?

2. Why do Mexican immigrants have a different assimilation process than immigrants in the past?

3. Why is the term "melting pot" inaccurate to describe American society today?

4. What is an example of a more meaningful term? Why is this term more meaningful?

5. What is Maria Jacinto afraid her children will learn from the Americans they associate with?

6. What is the most important value she wants her children to have?

## Vocabulary

ACTIVITY 3  **Academic Words** Write the letter of the correct definition for each word in **boldface** in each blank.

1. _____ Only half of the **estimated** number of people showed up to vote because of the awful weather.

2. _____ To **adapt** to life in a new country, it is necessary to keep an open mind.

3. _____ One **aspect** of America that immigrants often talk about is its freedom.

4. _____ The **process** of moving took many months.

5. _____ Parents usually **stress** that their children should get good grades.

6. _____ Maria Jacinto puts an **emphasis** on the Mexican tradition that family comes before money.

7. _____ There was no sign to **indicate** the name of the street.

8. _____ People who immigrate like to **maintain** contact with their families and friends back home.

9. _____ Because of the many opportunities in America for immigrants, it has become a land of **diversity**.

10. _____ She had already done her homework the **previous** night.

a. to give great importance to
b. to keep
c. a series of actions
d. to show or mark
e. the one coming before
f. to change so as to fit in
g. special attention
h. a way in which something can be viewed
i. judged in advance
j. many different kinds of people or things

**Vocabulary Analogy** An **analogy** is a relationship between two things. For example, you could say that the relationship between the verbs *leave* and *depart* is one of similarity. In other words, the two verbs have similar meanings.

Once you create a relationship between two things, it can sometimes be useful when writing to create the same kind of relationship between two other things. For example, you could say *leave* is to *depart* as *return* is to ___?___. To fill in the blank, you must understand that the relationship between *leave* and *depart* is one of similarity and then find a word that has a similar meaning to *return*.

Circle the letter of the word that best completes each analogy. If the first analogy shows similarity, then the second analogy should also show similarity. If the first analogy shows an opposite relationship, then the second analogy should also show an opposite relationship. Circle **S** for similar or **O** for opposite to describe the relationship. The first one is done for you.

1. leave : depart = return : _____

   (a.) come back     b. arrive     c. travel

   Relationship: (S)   O

2. end : conclusion = beginning : _____

   a. origin     b. border     c. avoid

   Relationship: S     O

3. avoid : resist = join : _____

   a. influence     b. connect     c. community

   Relationship: S     O

4. origin : end = blend : _____

   a. separate     b. stress     c. replace

   Relationship: S     O

5. entirely : completely = salad bowl : _____

   a. mainstream     b. melting pot     c. mosaic

   Relationship: S     O

6. common : group = different : _____

   a. influence     b. diversity     c. constant

   Relationship: S     O

# Composition Analysis

**Specific Actions and General Explanations**  One pattern of organizing information that writers use when they want to emphasize a point is the following:

Specific action or quote ———▶ General explanation

*or*

General explanation ———▶ Specific action or quote

The writer begins with some specific information, such as an action or a quote by a specific person, then explains the general meaning behind it. Or the writer begins with a general explanation, then gives specific information, such as an action or quote.

> **Specific action:** Maria Jacinto is making tortillas for the evening meal. She lives in a small house with her husband and five children in a neighborhood where most of the residents are Mexican immigrants. (paragraph 1)

> **General explanation:** ... immigrants now have a choice. They can resist Americanization if they want to. (paragraph 5)

**ACTIVITY 5**  Fill in the missing explanation or quote from Reading 1 in each pair below. There may be more than one correct answer.

1. **General explanation:** [Families such as the Jacintos] see their children assimilating, but often to aspects of American culture they do not agree with.

   **Specific quote:** _____

   _____

2. **Specific quote:** _____

   _____

   **General explanation:** ...[Jacinto] seems resistant to the idea of assimilating into U.S. society.

3. **Specific quote:** "In the Hispanic tradition, the family comes first, not money."

   **General explanation:** _____

   _____

# Writing 1

**ACTIVITY 6**  To help you prepare for the writing assignment in Activity 7, choose a topic and discuss the questions with a partner who has chosen the same topic as you. Write answers to the questions in your own words. You do not need to agree with your partner as long as you can give reasons for your answers.

Topic 1

1. In addition to placing too much importance on money, what other "immoral" things do you think Maria Jacinto's children might learn from Americans?

2. Do you think many American children are immoral? Why or why not?

3. What do you think the family "The Simpsons" represents?

Topic 2

1. Do you feel you are more American than your previous nationality?

2. Do you think you will become more American in the future?

3. Are you satisfied with how American you are right now? Why or why not?

4. Do you prefer to associate with family and friends who have the same nationality of origin as you? Why or why not?

**ACTIVITY 7**  **Writing Assignment** Write an essay about one of the following topics. Be sure to include in your paper all of the items in the checklist on page 142.

Topic 1

Maria Jacinto is worried that her children may learn from American kids to place too much importance on money. Are there other things that they may learn that she should worry about? Why? What do you think she means when she says, "Not all families here are like the Simpsons, are they?" Give reasons to support your answer.

Topic 2

Define how much you think you have become American. Give examples of changes you have made that make you more American. Do you have friends, neighbors, or relatives living near you that make you feel less American? Do you feel that you will be American when "your skin turns white and your hair turns blonde"? Give reasons to support your answer.

**Sentence Fragments**

A **fragment** is a piece of a sentence. It cannot stand alone the way a sentence does. It can be **a piece of a sentence that is separated from a main clause by a period.**

*Incorrect:* Maria Jacinto is making tortillas for the evening meal in the kitchen of the small house. Where she lives with her husband and five children.

*Correct:* Maria Jacinto is making tortillas for the evening meal in the kitchen of the small house where she lives with her husband and five children.

It can be **a piece of a sentence that lacks a main verb.**

*Incorrect:* To assimilate into a new culture.

*Correct:* To assimilate into a new culture takes time.

Or it can be **a piece of a sentence that lacks a main verb and a subject.**

*Incorrect:* When my skin turns white and my hair turns blonde.

*Correct:* I'll be an American when my skin turns white and my hair turns blonde.

---

**ACTIVITY 8**  Each of the following items contains one complete sentence and one sentence fragment. Circle the letter of the one that is a complete sentence. Then underline the subject of the complete sentence <u>once</u> and the main verb <u>twice</u>.

1. (a.) Coming to the end of the road, <u>we</u> <u>realized</u> we had to go back.

   b. Coming to the end of the road, realizing we had to go back.

2. a. After taking the test which was very long and difficult.

   b. The test which I took was very long and difficult.

3. a. Maria Jacinto and her husband, who moved to the United States ten years ago to find jobs in the meatpacking industry.

   b. Ten years ago Maria Jacinto and her husband moved to the United States to find jobs in the meatpacking industry.

4. a. All around the world American culture influences people.

   b. American culture influencing people all around the world.

5. a. Jacinto becoming a U.S. citizen last April, but not feeling like an American.

   b. Even after becoming a U.S. citizen, Jacinto does not feel like an American.

6. a. When we returned home after five years, there was nothing left of the life we knew before.

   b. Returning home after five years was nothing left of the life we knew before.

7. a. Where we live almost all of our neighbors and friends are Spanish speakers.

   b. Where almost all of our neighbors and friends who live near us are Spanish speakers.

For each of the following sentences, decide if the sentence is complete or incomplete. If it is complete, write **C** in the blank. If it is incomplete, write **IC** and correct it. Be sure you do not change the meaning.

1. _____ Never before have so many immigrants resisted a "melting pot" assimilation.

2. _____ The houses on that street are all the same. With no difference except the color.

3. _____ My family standing beside me. I said my goodbyes and boarded the plane to come to America.

4. _____ Leaving the country where I had lived my whole life. I thought back on how I had come to the decision to go.

5. _____ I could not have imagined what I was in for. America was different in every way from the small village in Vietnam where I grew up.

6. _____ Stop, I kept telling myself. These impressions are all coming too fast.

7. _____ Talking as quickly as I could. I explained why I had called.

8. _____ Just speaking the language well is not enough. To succeed in a new country.

## Rewriting 1

**Peer Activity** Trade your paper from Activity 7 with another student. Read your partner's paper. Go back to the title. Does the title correctly predict the main point of the composition? Next find the two or three supporting points for the main idea. Number them Point 1, Point 2, etc. Then find at least one example or detail to support each point and number them Detail 1, Detail 2, etc., to correspond to each point. In other words, Point 1 should have a Detail 1, Point 2, a Detail 2, and so on as in the example below from Reading 1.

Point 1

The experiences of the Jacinto family are in many ways typical of the slow process of assimilation that brings many immigrants into the American mainstream.

Detail 1

"I think I'm still a Mexican," [says Maria Jacinto].

Talk to your partner about what you found and help him or her make any necessary changes.

**On Your Own** Review your partner's notes, your partner's comments, and your teacher's feedback on the first draft of your composition. Use the Composition Evaluation Sheet (from Appendix 1) that your teacher returned to you to see specifically what you need to improve. Then consider the questions in the checklist below. Finally, rewrite your paper to make it clearer and more meaningful.

## ✔CHECKLIST

### Content

Does your composition have a title that predicts your main point?

Does your thesis statement address the topic?

Do you give explanations for specific actions or quotes you use?

### Organization

Is your point of view about the topic clear in your thesis statement?

Does your essay stay focused on the point of view in your thesis statement?

Do you give adequate support for your point of view through examples and explanation?

Does your conclusion restate the main idea in the thesis statement?

### Grammar

Do you avoid using any sentence fragments?

## PART 2

## Reading 2:  Extending the Topic Reading

This is the story of a young Norwegian student nurse. She feels that her interests and emotions are as American as those of anyone around her, and yet she feels different in a way that she does not understand. She returns after many years to Norway for a visit and only then does she realize to her surprise that there she does not feel different. She feels at home.

As you read the story, think about the events in her life that make her feel different and imagine yourself in her situation. How does it feel? You will use your thoughts later in this chapter.

 ## I Was Home

1    Joining the military as an Army student nurse, taking the oath[8] under the flag that day, I felt a deep joy that went beyond the honor and responsibility of the moment. I realized that not only would I serve and defend America, but also that the military would take care of me.

2    I now had a credible future. I went about my work with new hope and purpose. But that vague question lingered: Why did I feel alienated[9] from my peers? Why did I feel different? Though taller, I looked the same, dressed the same, took the same courses, enjoyed the same music. In fact, I often sang and played folk music with my classmates—music of The Weavers and The Kingston Trio that we all loved. The lyrics[10] moved me just as they did everyone else. Still, I felt different. When people older than myself entered the room, I stood up. This, appropriate in the recruiting

---

[8] *oath:* promise
[9] *alienated:* made to feel strange and different
[10] *lyrics:* the words of a song

office,[11] was out of place on campus, but I did it automatically. In greeting others, I always shook hands (which women never did in those days). I held the door open for people, even my classmates, but felt awkward if they did the same for me (the tallest should always hold the door). These behaviors came naturally. They felt right to me—and yet they also made me feel out of place. What was wrong?

3    When I was a child in Norway I never felt different from others. That came when we moved to America. It occurred to me that I might find some answers in Norway, so I saved my money for a trip back. My grandmother was getting old, and I had yet to fulfill my childhood promise to visit. So in August 1962, I returned to Norway for the first time in eleven years. The trip was more wonderful and meaningful than I had ever imagined it would be. By the time the airport taxi pulled up in front of my grandmother's apartment building in Oslo, I was so excited to be home, I ran out of the cab, burst through the entrance, and raced up the five flights of stairs, so oblivious[12] to everything but my destination that I dropped packages the entire way up the staircase. When I reached the door, grandmother embraced me happily, crying, *"Kjaere Grethemor velkommen hjem."* Behind me, laughing and beaming, my aunt followed, her arms loaded with all the gifts I had dropped along the way. The sweet pleasure of belonging, just as I was, without any need to be otherwise, returned after an eleven-year absence.

4    I spent weeks visiting with relatives and friends, traveling to the countryside, drinking in all that was familiar and loved, savoring the words *Jeg er hjemme*—I am home. I began to notice something remarkable: everywhere I went, young people stood up when their elders entered the room; women always shook hands in greeting and held the door open for others. This etiquette[13] was expected and proper. I realized that rather than being different, with its implication that this was somehow wrong, I had been doing exactly what I was supposed to be doing. I was being Norwegian. There was nothing wrong with me. I decided that all the feelings of uncertainty, loneliness, and alienation I experienced as a teenager and a college student were explained by the fact that I'd been born and raised in Norway, and was Norwegian. My exoneration.[14] I didn't have to be worried about a mysterious reason why I felt different in America. Here I was like everyone else. I fit in, I was home.

Excerpt from the book, *Serving in Silence*, by Margarethe Cammermeyer.

11 *recruiting office:* place where people join the military
12 *oblivious:* lacking awareness
13 *etiquette:* the rules of proper behavior
14 *exoneration:* the state of being relieved from blame

ACTIVITY 12    **Discussion** Discuss these questions with your classmates.

1. As a student nurse, why was Margarethe Cammermeyer happy and unhappy at the same time?

2. Why did she feel different from others around her? Give two examples.

3. What did she decide to do to try to understand her feelings?

4. What did she discover in Norway that made her feel better?

5. How do you think she felt when she returned to the United States after her visit home? Why?

**ACTIVITY 13**

**Group Activity** On a separate piece of paper, write two things that have happened to you that suddenly made you feel alienated from people in the United States. Tell what happened and tell why you think you felt bad. When you have finished, form a group with 3–4 other students and put your papers in a pile.

Each student should choose a paper that is not his or her own and read the two situations to the group. The group should try to guess who the paper belongs to. When the papers are identified by their owners, discuss the situations. Are some situations similar? How are they similar?

## Vocabulary

**ACTIVITY 14**

**Academic Words** Complete the paragraph below with the correct forms of the words in the list. Be sure to use the correct forms. You will not use all of the words.

| Words | Meanings |
|---|---|
| **appropriate** | correct and fitting |
| **automatically** | done easily without thinking |
| **credible** | believable and acceptable |
| **embraced** | hugged strongly |
| **fulfill** | to accomplish |
| **occur** | to happen |
| **peer** | a person of equal age or class |
| **staircase** | a flight of stairs |
| **savoring** | enjoying to the fullest |
| **vague** | not clear or well-defined |

Two summers ago I took an important trip which (1) _____ a dream for me. I was excited to be going to Denmark, the country where I was born. I stayed for several days with my cousin and his wife who both (2) _____ me warmly when I came. They have a house with a (3) _____ going up the middle in the countryside outside of Copenhagen. I (4) _____ the sights such as the thatched roofs[15] and tidy little farms as well as the sounds of the language I had heard in my home as a child. I felt a (5) _____ sense of belonging that made everything seem (6) _____ even though I had not visited for many years, because I ate food that my mother used to make and heard words all around me that I had spoken long ago. Also, my relatives were so kind to me that I

[15] *thatched roofs:* roofs made of tightly packed straw

(7) _____ felt accepted as part of the family. As I left, I could only hope that they will find it (8) _____ to visit me in the United States so I can show them the same kindness.

## Composition Analysis

ACTIVITY 15 **Finding Support Sentences** In the Composition Analysis section on page 138, you learned how general explanations support specific actions and quotes to strengthen main points. For each sentence from Reading 2 below, decide if it describes a specific action or gives a general explanation. Write **SA** for specific action or **GE** for general explanation in the blank. Then find a sentence in Reading 2 that supports either the specific action (with a general explanation) or the general explanation (with a specific action). The first one is done for you.

1. \_\_*SA*\_\_ ... Taking the oath under the flag, ... I felt a deep joy that went beyond the honor and responsibility of the moment. (paragraph 1)

   **Support Sentence:** *I realized that not only would I serve and defend America, but also that the military would take care of me.*

2. _____ Why did I feel alienated from my peers? (paragraph 2)

   **Support Sentence:** _____

   _____

3. _____ The sweet pleasure of belonging, just as I was, returned after an eleven-year absence. (paragraph 3)

   **Support Sentence:** _____

   _____

4. _____ Everywhere I went, young people stood up when their elders entered the room; women always shook hands in greeting and held the door open for others. (paragraph 4)

   **Support Sentence:** _____

   _____

5. _____ I decided that all the feelings of uncertainty, loneliness, and alienation I experienced as a teenager and a college student were explained by the fact that I'd been born and raised in Norway, and was Norwegian. (paragraph 4)

   **Support Sentence:** _____

   _____

# Making Connections

ACTIVITY 16 In Reading 1, we learn the following things about Maria Jacinto:

1. She does not feel ready to accept American values and be an American.

2. She does not speak English.

3. She lives in a neighborhood of Mexican immigrants like herself.

4. She wants to preserve her family's Mexican heritage.

5. She worries about the values that her children are learning from Americans.

In Reading 2, we learn the following things about Margarethe Cammermeyer:

6. She feels in most ways like an American.

7. She lives among Americans and enjoys the same things Americans do.

8. Her feelings of being different from Americans surprise and confuse her.

9. She wants to be an American and not feel different.

10. She feels it is important to understand her heritage.

For each of the following statements, decide if it agrees with the point of view of Maria Jacinto, Margarethe Cammermeyer, or both. Write **J** for Jacinto, **C** for Cammermeyer, or **JC** for both. Then choose one or more reasons for your answer from the list of items 1–10 above and write the numbers in the blank. When you are finished, form a group of three or four students and discuss your answers.

1. _____ I think it is important for immigrants to preserve their cultural heritage.

   Reasons: _____

2. _____ Someday maybe I will be an American.

   Reasons: _____

3. _____ My neighbors are much like me.

   Reasons: _____

4. _____ I need to make a trip back to my country so that I can understand my feelings.

   Reasons: _____

5. _____ I don't agree with some of the values that Americans have.

   Reasons: _____

6. _____ It is not always easy to adjust to life in America.

   Reasons: _____

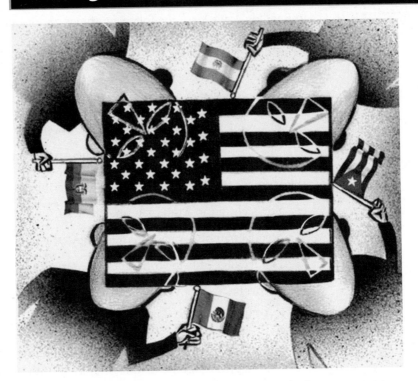

 **America: No Longer the Melting Pot**

1    Assimilation in America has historically been a great success. But let's think about what assimilation really means. Most Americans believe that, to assimilate, immigrants must give up their home cultures and conform to the ways of native-born Americans. This, however, is not the American style of assimilation that we see both past and present.

2    It is not surprising that Americans think immigrants must change their ways in order to fit in because this is what often happens in other countries. For example, the French force Muslim women who immigrate from North Africa to give up wearing their chadors.[16] But this kind of assimilation as a rejection[17] of immigrant culture is not the American style of assimilation. An American attitude of flexibility[18] allows immigrants to preserve much of their own culture while creating a new American identity. It also allows the United States to preserve its national unity even as waves of immigrants come from all over the world.

3    The term often used to describe American assimilation is "melting pot." When we really think about this term, we see that it means a place where people melt together. This concept leads to one important conclusion: everyone changes. Immigrants and non-immigrants alike blend into one homogenized[19] substance. No one is different from anyone else and no one is the same as before the process began. However, if we look around, we can easily see that Hispanic, Asian, European

---

16 *chador:* a cloth used as a covering by Muslim and Hindu women
17 *rejection:* a failure to accept something
18 *flexible:* responsive to change
19 *homogenized:* different elements blended into a uniform mixture

and any other immigrants are not at all the same. They have their own cultural attitudes and behaviors and often they have their own neighborhoods. Non-immigrant Americans, lacking the immigrant experience, clearly are not the same as immigrants either although they may eat and drink differently, socialize differently, and entertain themselves differently because of immigrant influence.

4    Therefore, we are now seeing some new terms that critics of the "melting pot" idea find more accurate. These include "rainbow coalition," "gorgeous mosaic," and "salad bowl." Unlike the "melting pot" metaphor, all of these names suggest that the immigrant groups in the United States may live side by side successfully without changing their identity. In addition, they also suggest a unity and strength based on the idea that a "salad" is something greater than the sum of its greens.[20]

5    So if we consider the American model, we could say that assimilation refers to the participation in a civic unity that also allows personal freedom. Therein lies its success. For over two hundred years, America has been a culturally unified nation which has grown to three hundred million people drawn from every corner of the earth.

Excerpt from the book, *Assimilation, American Style*, by Peter Salins.

[20] *greens:* the substance of a salad

## Composition Analysis

**A Definition Essay**   In a **definition essay**, as the name suggests, a place, thing, idea, or experience is defined. In Reading 3, Salins defines one view of assimilation. He organizes his definition into stating both what he thinks assimilation is and what it is not. An outline of the information presented might look like this:

I.   Assimilation, American style, is different from what people think

   A. What American assimilation is *not*

      1. immigrants giving up their home cultures and conforming to the ways of native-born Americans.

      2. a melting pot

         a. because not all people in America are the same

         b. because native-born Americans are not changed beyond recognition by immigration

   B. What American assimilation *is*

      1. an attitude of flexibility that has allowed the United States to preserve its national unity

      2. attractive because ethnic groups live side by side harmoniously without altering their identity

         a. a rainbow coalition

         b. a gorgeous mosaic

         c. a salad bowl

An outline like this is a useful tool for understanding the relationship between ideas in a reading. It also summarizes the important points and puts them all in one small space so they are easy to remember. You might write an outline based on a reading after you have studied it to help you remember the important points.

You can also use an outline to organize your ideas before you write a composition. This gives you a kind of road map to follow so you present your ideas in a logical way. It also helps you to avoid leaving anything out. Your teacher may suggest that you make an outline of your points before you write a composition.

**ACTIVITY 17** | Fill in the missing information from Reading 1 to complete the following outline.

I. Changes in assimilation include less blending and more separateness

    A. Causes of the change in assimilation

        1. More immigrants than ever before come from a single country—Mexico

        2. More immigrants than ever before speak one language—Spanish

        3. _____

    B. Results of the change in assimilation

        1. Mexican immigrants have the opportunity to develop a greater connection with each other than previous immigrants had

            a. _____

            b. They worry about the American influence on their children

                i. _____

                ii. The Simpsons

        2. Assimilation no longer means following the ways of the native born

            a. _____

            b. _____

# Writing 2

To help you prepare for the writing assignment in Activity 19, choose a topic and discuss the questions with a partner who has chosen the same topic as you. Write answers to the questions in your own words. You do not need to agree with your partner as long as you can give reasons for your answers.

Topic 1

1. Do you think more immigrants prefer the "salad bowl" way of assimilation to the "melting pot" way?

2. Tell your partner a story about yourself or someone else who has followed the "salad bowl" method of assimilation.

Topic 2

1. Tell your partner how much you are becoming part of the culture around you and how much you prefer to stay separate.

2. Are you satisfied with your level of assimilation?

3. Are you part of a "salad bowl" or a "melting pot"? Explain.

ACTIVITY 19 **Writing Assignment** Write a **definition essay** about one of the following topics. Be sure to include in your paper all of the items in the checklist on page 155. Make an outline of your ideas before you write your essay.

Topic 1

Give an example from your own reading or experience that supports the "salad bowl" definition of assimilation in Reading 3. Show how the details of your example support the main ideas of the definition in the reading.

Topic 2

Define your own personal assimilation process. How much are you blending in and how much are you separate from the culture around you? Do you feel comfortable with your level of assimilation? Are the details of your experience similar to the main ideas in Reading 3?

# Grammar

| | |
|---|---|
| **Parallel Structure** | **Parallel structure** means using the same pattern of words, phrases, or clauses to give two or more ideas equal emphasis and importance. These structures must have the same pattern to be grammatically correct. Parallel structures are usually joined by periods or commas and *and* or *or*. |

> *Correct:* I enjoy **dancing, singing,** and **playing** the piano.
> *Incorrect:* I enjoy **dancing, singing,** and **to play** the piano.

In the first sentence, the pattern is the use of gerunds to describe activities. The second sentence is incorrect because the pattern is mixed—it has two gerunds and one infinitive.

In the following sentence from Reading 3, we see a different pattern.

> I was taller, but I **looked** the same, **dressed** the same, **took** the same courses, **enjoyed** the same music.

All of the items in this sentence are phrases with the past tense of a verb. In addition, each of the phrases includes the word *same*.

---

**ACTIVITY 20**  Use the following words and phrases to create sentences with **parallel structure**. Verbs in phrases are in the base form, so you need to choose verb tenses. There is more than one correct answer. The first one is done for you.

1. a lot of homework to do—a paper, twenty math problems, a chapter in biology

   *I have a lot of homework to do. I have a paper to write, twenty math problems to solve, and a chapter of biology to read.*

2. Margarethe Cammermeyer—Army recruit, student nurse, Norwegian

   _____

   _____

3. Margarethe was excited when she arrived at her grandmother's apartment building—ran out of the cab, burst through the entrance, race up the five flights of stairs

   _____

   _____

4. While Margarethe was running upstairs, her aunt—laugh, beam, pick up Margarethe's packages from the stairs

   _____

   _____

5. Assimilation to a new country means more than—speak the language fluently, get a good job, have good relationships with the people, enjoy the food

_____

_____

6. Mexican immigrants in the United States can, if they choose—eat Mexican food, speak Spanish, have Mexican neighbors

_____

_____

Now write a sentence of your own using parallel structure.

7. _____

_____

**ACTIVITY 21**   Find the eight parallel structure errors in the following paragraph and correct them.

Assimilation is not an easy process. It may begin with some relatively small decisions like where to buy food, where to find transportation, and how being friendly to other people. Other decisions such as find affordable housing, getting a good job, and locate good schools may be more difficult. A still more difficult decision for each individual is figuring out just how much assimilation is the right amount. Considerations might include concern for lose too much home country identity, fear of connect to certain undesirable aspects of American culture, and worry about make many uncomfortable changes. Assimilation does not happen all at once. It happens in steps, usually when you are busy doing something else like work or cooking or shop or just talking.

# Rewriting 2

ACTIVITY 22 **Peer Activity** Trade your paper from Activity 19 with another student. Read your partner's paper. Then look at your partner's outline. Does the thesis statement include the same point as the most general point (I) in the outline? If so, write **I** next to the thesis statement. In the example below, the thesis statement and Point I of the outline are about the same idea.

### Thesis Statement

*I*

> Most Americans believe that for immigrants to assimilate, they must give up their home cultures and conform to the ways of native-born Americans. This, however, is not the American style of assimilation that we can see both in the past and the present.

### Outline, Point I

> I. Assimilation, American style, is different from what people think

Next, find two or three statements in the composition that support this thesis statement. Number them 1, 2, etc., as in the example below from Reading 3.

> But this kind of assimilation as a rejection of immigrant culture is not the American style of assimilation. *1* An American attitude of flexibility allows immigrants to preserve much of their own culture while creating a new American identity. *2* It also allows the United States to preserve its national unity even as waves of immigrants come from all over the world.

Talk to your partner about what you found and help him or her make any necessary changes that would clarify his or her main points.

**ACTIVITY 23**   **On Your Own**  Review your partner's notes, your partner's comments, and your teacher's feedback on the first draft of your composition. Use the Composition Evaluation Sheet (from Appendix 1) that your teacher returned to you to see specifically what you need to improve. Then consider the questions in the checklist below. Finally, rewrite your paper to make it clearer and more meaningful.

**✔CHECKLIST**

**Content**

Does your thesis statement address the question in the topic?

Are the points in your outline the same as the points in your composition?

Do you have any irrelevant sentences?

Is your composition interesting?

**Organization**

Does your essay stay focused on the definition or point of view in your thesis statement?

Do you give adequate support for your point of view through details and reasons?

Does your conclusion summarize your points?

**Grammar**

Do you have any sentence fragments?

Do you use correct parallel structure?

## Internet Activities

For additional activities related to this chapter, go to elt.thomson.com/catalyst.

## Exploring the Topic

ACTIVITY 1

**Discussion** It is the extreme danger in her homeland that forces her to leave and become a refugee. However, with the pain and the risk of departure comes the gratitude that another country welcomes her. With this gratitude, however, comes the feeling that she does not automatically belong; that she must prove she deserves the favor she has received. Her accomplishments and a place to call home are her rewards.

In groups of 3–4, discuss the following ideas and questions. Then share your ideas with the class.

1. What makes you feel like you belong to a place? Give some examples.

2. What experiences have you had that made you long for something familiar to you?

3. What is the one thing about American culture you find most difficult to deal with?

4. Do you feel a strong sense of responsibility to succeed in the United States? Explain.

157

## PART 1

## Reading 1: Personal Experience Reading

This is the story of Nola Kambanda's entry into the United States from Burundi where she and her family were refugees.[1] Her immediate feelings as soon as she landed were a mixture of amazement and determination—amazement at the speed and complexity of life around her and determination to succeed in a strange new country with much to offer.

As you read the story, think about the specific causes of her amazement and her determination to succeed. You will use your thoughts later in this chapter.

## My New World Journey

1    The anticipation of coming to America with all of its greatness was simply overwhelming. When I came to Los Angeles from Burundi,[2] a place that was so very different in every way from the United States, I was in complete awe. It made me feel like a toddler[3] in a toy store. I was unable to decide which adventure to experience first. The first thing I noticed was the speed with which everything was going. It seemed too fast. The people all rushed around and no one was looking anywhere except where they were going. The cars also moved too fast. There were too many lights, too many buttons to press, too many escalators.[4] I was suddenly asking myself if these people ever stopped to talk to one another. The longing to be

[1] *refugee:* a person who leaves a country because of war, political pressure, or religious persecution
[2] *Burundi:* a country in Central Africa
[3] *toddler:* a very young child
[4] *escalator:* a stairway consisting of moving steps

back home suddenly came upon me. The need for some kind of familiarity was so strong and yet I had just stepped off the plane.

2     I think all refugees grow up with the understanding that you do not automatically belong somewhere. You always have to prove yourself. You have to earn your place in the society that has so kindly allowed you the freedom of life. When I was growing up, it was just assumed that we would do well in school. There was no room for failure, for being anything other than the best. I, like all my siblings, excelled in my academics. I left Bujumbura, the capital city, to complete my secondary education at an all-girls boarding school in Kiganda, a small countryside town. My first year at school in Kiganda was pleasant enough. My second year, however, was another story.

3     The territory of Central Africa where I am from is full of tribal warfare.[5] The hatred between the two main tribes in both Burundi and Rwanda has existed for a hundred years and is most likely far from over. It is hard to change when you know no other way of life.

4     I suppose that this was true of the young Hutu[6] student at my boarding school who was plotting[7] to kill me, a Tutsi.[8] Actually, she and a small group of her Hutu friends were planning to kill all the Tutsi students. Mine was first on a list of over thirty names that the administration discovered. The girls were threatened with expulsion[9] and their murderous plans quickly came to an end. But for me, it was a serious reminder that I was a refugee and that meant I was never safe. I was never truly home. When I told my parents what had happened, their reaction only fixed this in my mind. "This is what you have to live with, Nola," they said. "This is who you are."

5     So there I was years later standing outside the Los Angeles International Airport watching cars and buses of all sizes and shapes drive by. I thought about how I had reached this point in my life. I realized the sacrifice that not only my parents but also my siblings were making to send me out here. I was the first one of all seven of my parents' children to move so far away from Burundi. I should have felt privileged. I should have been excited and on top of the world about coming to America—the richest and most technologically advanced country of them all.

6     However, a sense of guilt was washing over me. I kept thinking of the economic weight it would place on my father. I felt this was too large for him to bear in order to accommodate just one child. This guilt brought on a tremendous sense of responsibility for me. Even more so than in Burundi, failure was unacceptable. I could not fail here in America. I was going to have to be the best. I was going to have to do extremely well in school so that I could go on to get a decent job. Then I would be able to contribute financially to my family's well-being.

*(continued in Reading 2)*

Excerpt by Nola Kambanda from the book, *Becoming American: Personal Essays by First Generation Immigrant Women*, edited by Meri Nana-Ama Danquah.

[5] *tribal warfare:* fighting between tribes
[6] *Hutu:* a member of the Hutu tribe in Central Africa that is at war with the Tutsis
[7] *plotting:* planning
[8] *Tutsi:* a member of the Tutsi tribe in Central Africa that is at war with the Hutus
[9] *expulsion:* being forcefully sent away

**Discussion** Discuss these questions with your classmates.

1. What are two feelings Nola Kambanda, the author, had when she landed in Los Angeles? Give an example of each.

2. According to the author, what do all refugees understand?

3. Why did Kambanda feel she had to do well in school?

4. Why did the Hutu girls want to kill Kambanda and all of the other Tutsi students?

5. What did this death scare remind Kambanda of?

6. Is Kambanda excited to be in America? Why or why not?

7. What feeling does she have when she thinks about her father and her siblings? Why?

## Vocabulary

ACTIVITY 3 **Academic Words** Write the letter of the correct definition for each word in **boldface** in the blank.

_____ 1. Children are usually full of **anticipation** at Christmas time.

_____ 2. I **excelled** in math, but I never did well in music or sports.

_____ 3. My new washing machine is **technologically** advanced. It uses much less water and energy than my old one.

_____ 4. When you don't get enough sleep, you are more **susceptible** to illness.

_____ 5. He felt **privileged** to receive an award for the work he did for that organization.

_____ 6. I hope the weather will be **decent** for the picnic tomorrow.

_____ 7. In her last year of college, she was more interested in music than **academics**.

_____ 8. It takes **tremendous** energy to raise children.

_____ 9. Teachers must **accommodate** the individual needs of students as much as possible.

a. did very well
b. resulting from scientific or industrial progress
c. excited expectation
d. a great quantity
e. a source of great worry or stress
f. courses and studies
g. honored
h. easily affected by
i. to do a favor or service for
j. of good quality
k. surprise and wonder
l. supposed
m. people who manage or govern an institution

_____ 10. He **assumed** that he deserved a raise when he asked his boss to give him one.

_____ 11. I was in **awe** of snow the first time I saw it.

_____ 12. The **administration** of my school will not allow students to take a final exam early.

## Composition Analysis

**Levels of Generality** Good writers use several levels of generality ranging from very general to very specific in order to make their points. Look at the example below. Notice how the more specific statements add clear concrete detail to the most general statement. Level 2 expands the meaning of Level 1, and Level 3 expands the meaning of Level 2 and Level 1. Similarly, Level 1 connects Levels 2 and 3 to an important general point or main idea.

**Level 1** (most general): Kambanda was in complete awe when she came to the United States.

**Level 2** (next most general): The first thing she noticed was the speed with which everything was going.

**Level 3** (most specific): The people all rushed around and no one was looking anywhere except where they were going.

ACTIVITY 4

**A.** Choose statements from the following list to fill in the missing levels in 1–3 below.

Kambanda feels a sense of responsibility to do extremely well in college.

Kambanda is a refugee and never feels completely safe.

Kambanda came to Los Angeles from Burundi.

1. **Level 1:** Tribal warfare exists between two major tribes in Central Africa.

   **Level 2:** _____

   **Level 3:** A Hutu girl at Kambanda's boarding school wanted to kill her.

2. **Level 1:** Kambanda and her family were refugees and believed in a better life.

   **Level 2:** Her family sent her to the United States for the opportunity to continue her education.

   **Level 3:** _____

3. **Level 1:** _____

   **Level 2:** Her first impression was that everything seemed to move too fast in America.

   **Level 3:** There were too many lights, too many buttons to press, too many escalators.

**B.** Put the following statements in order from general to specific as in numbers 1–3 above.

I could never have imagined so many cars, trucks, and buses moving on one road at one time.

For example, I had never seen a freeway with four lanes of traffic going in each direction.

My first impression of America was how large everything was.

**Level 1:** _____

**Level 2:** _____

**Level 3:** _____

# Writing 1

**ACTIVITY 5**

To help you prepare for the writing assignment in Activity 6, choose a topic and discuss the questions with a partner who has chosen the same topic as you. Write answers to the questions in your own words. You do not need to agree with your partner as long as you can give reasons for your answers.

Topic 1

1. Look at paragraphs 1, 5, and 6 of Reading 1. Of all of Kambanda's impressions, which one do you think she felt most strongly?

2. Why do you think this impression was so strong?

Topic 2

1. Tell your partner about the one impression of the United States you felt most strongly when you first arrived.

2. Why do you think this impression was so strong?

3. Was this similar to any of Kambanda's impressions?

**Writing Assignment** Write an essay about one of the following topics. Be sure to include in your paper all of the items in the checklist on page 166.

Topic 1

Describe what you think Kambanda felt most strongly on the day of her arrival in the United States. What other feelings did she have? Why do you think this feeling was stronger than others? Use examples from the reading to support your opinion.

Topic 2

Describe the feeling you had most strongly about the United States when you first arrived. Why do you think you felt this so strongly? Did Kambanda have a similar feeling? Use examples from your experience to support your points.

# Grammar

## Adjective Clauses

**Adjective clauses** are clauses that identify or provide specific information about nouns (or pronouns). The adjective clause directly follows the noun (or pronoun) it refers to. These clauses begin with a relative pronoun such as *who, that, which, whose, where,* or *when.*

Some relative pronouns are **subject relative pronouns**. A subject relative pronoun is the subject of the adjective clause.

*subject relative pronoun*    *verb*

The United States is a country **which** attracts a lot of immigrants.

The adjective clause gives more information about the noun *country.*

Other relative pronouns are **object relative pronouns**. An object relative pronoun is the object of the adjective clause.

*object relative pronoun*    *verb*

The awe **that** Kambanda felt in the Los Angeles airport was overwhelming.

The adjective clause gives us more information about the noun *awe.*

In informal speech or writing, when you use *who* or *that* to refer to people, you can leave out these relative pronouns. When you use *which* or *that* to refer to things, you can also leave out these relative pronouns.

Look at the following examples:

**Subject Relative Pronoun Adjective Clauses**

**who/that**    refers to people (*that* is less formal)
Kambanda saw people in the airport **who** were all rushing around.
My father was the one person **that** made me know I had to succeed.

**whose**    refers to possession
Kambanda, **whose** parents were political refugees from Rwanda, was born in Burundi.

### Object Relative Pronoun Adjective Clauses

**that/which** **refers to things** (Use *that* in restrictive clauses and *which* in non-restrictive clauses.)

I was first on a list of over thirty students **that** some Tutsi classmates wanted to kill.

Kambanda came to a new country, **which** she found different in every way from Burundi.

**that** **can also refer to people** (*that* is less formal than whom)

This is the woman **that** I want to marry.

**where** **refers to place**

Los Angeles was the place **where** Kambanda entered the United States.

**when** **refers to time**

The moment of arrival in the United States is a time **when** many immigrants feel overwhelmed.

---

**ACTIVITY 7** — Fill in each blank with a relative pronoun from the list: *who, that, which, whose, where,* or *when.* If no relative pronoun is needed write **0**. There may be more than one correct answer.

1. We visited the house _____ my family used to live.

2. Of all her siblings, Nola was the one _____ came to the United States to study.

3. During the time _____ Kambanda was standing in the Los Angeles airport, she was overwhelmed with the speed of everything.

4. Immigrants _____ families do not come with them often suffer much homesickness.

5. If I can't finish my project at work in time to go on vacation next week, then we'll have to go another time _____ I don't have quite so much to do.

6. The day _____ I arrived in the United States was one of the happiest days of my life.

7. I can't believe our teacher didn't tell us until today that tomorrow we're going to have a test _____ covers three chapters in our book.

8. Please take my homework to class with you _____ you go because I have to work late today so I will be absent.

Write an adjective clause in each blank beginning with the given relative pronoun. The first one is done for you.

1. The child **whose** _mother walked out of the room_ started to cry.

2. The car **that** _____ _____ was involved in an accident.

3. The season **when** _____ _____ is the summer.

4. The teacher **who** _____ _____ won an award for her outstanding contribution to the school.

5. The movie we went to last night, **which** _____ _____, put me to sleep almost as soon as it started.

6. The rain, **which** _____ _____, had turned the road into a river of mud.

7. The girls at Kambanda's school **who** _____ _____ were threatened with expulsion.

8. At 7:30 PM, **when** _____ _____, my sister wasn't there.

9. A student in my English class **whose** _____ _____ showed me a very effective way to learn new vocabulary.

## Rewriting 1

**ACTIVITY 9**  **Peer Activity**  Trade your paper from Activity 6 with another student. Read your partner's paper. If the writer wrote about Topic 1, write at the top of the page the first sentence of the description of Topic 1. If the writer wrote about Topic 2, write at the top of the page the first sentence of the description of Topic 2. Then read the thesis statement and write the name of the strong feeling. Next, circle the two or more reasons that support the answer in the thesis statement. If your partner has not given the necessary information, help him or her make needed changes.

**ACTIVITY 10**  **On Your Own**  Review your partner's notes, your partner's comments, and your teacher's feedback on the first draft of your composition. Use the Composition Evaluation Sheet (from Appendix 1) that your teacher returned to you to see specifically what you need to improve. Then consider the questions in the checklist below. Finally, rewrite your paper to make it clearer and more meaningful.

---

**CHECKLIST**

**Content**
Does your thesis statement answer the question in the topic?
Do you support your reasons with examples?
Do you stick to the topic and avoid irrelevant sentences?

**Organization**
Do you give at least two reasons for your answer in the body of your composition?
Do you give details from at least two levels of generality?
Does your conclusion summarize the answer in your thesis statement?

**Grammar**
Do you use adjective clauses correctly?

---

## PART 2

## *Reading 2:* **Extending the Topic Reading**

The amazement that Nola Kambanda experienced on her first day in America continues and leads day by day to many adjustments. All of this is not easy, but the result is that America is becoming home to her a little at a time.

As you read this part of the story, think about what the most important ingredient of home is for Nola. You will use your thoughts later in this chapter.

7    The world I eventually came to know in America, in Los Angeles, and in the home where I was living was both comfortable and complicated. My new family welcomed me warmly and never made me feel like I didn't fit in just right. In short, they made it as painless as possible for me to merge into their way of life. Still there were many things I had to learn. The differences in our cultures and lifestyles[10] continued to display themselves as the days went by. Everything was rushed, was too this or too that, was always being pushed to the extreme. There just seemed to be so much information to recall. Where had all the simple things gone?

8    I had used a telephone plenty of times before and I had always thought of it as a pretty basic unit. You pick up the phone, you dial who you're calling, they answer, and you talk. If someone is calling you, the phone rings, you answer it, and you talk. No interruptions, no complexities. Until I learned that there was such a thing as call waiting. And then three-way calling. And call forwarding.[11] And single telephone units with multiple lines. What was all this? Was it all really necessary?

9    Then for labor saving,[12] there was, for instance, the washing machine. I had neither seen nor used one before. You put your dirty clothes and some soap into a machine, close the lid, press a button and within minutes, your clothes are done—clean and ready to be placed in yet another machine to be dried!?! Back at home, in Burundi, we would put our dirty clothes in a basin, soak them a bit, hand wash them with soap, and then hang them up to line dry. I will admit that the American way is definitely more convenient. However, there is a care that I like to put into the cleaning of my clothes, those things that cover and protect my body. So I still most often find myself hand washing.

[10] *lifestyle:* a way of living that reflects the attitudes and values of a person or group
[11] *call forwarding:* a phone feature which can be set so calls automatically go to a different number
[12] *labor saving:* creating less work, or making something easier

10    Only recently did I realize that the majority of all these cultural contrasts[13] came from the same root—the concept of time. Americans have a way of wanting to accomplish as much as possible in as little time as possible. Even something as sacred as eating. Fast food. It was amazing how many fast-food restaurants there were in Los Angeles, even in just our small neighborhood. Everyone ate at fast-food restaurants. I noticed how many ate while driving or being driven. I had not seen anything like this in my country. We ate three meals a day—breakfast, lunch, and dinner; and this was rarely done outside of either your own home or someone else's home. Eating out was a very formal affair. People didn't go to eat out by themselves. It was what you did in large numbers, something the whole family did together. Regardless of whether people ate in the home or out, dining required time. Food was never fast.

11    Sometimes I do think about going back home. I think about the rewards of having an extended family and a local community that needs my involvement. I think about finding a mate[14] who will be able to accept and relate to all aspects of my background and my culture. I have not yet been able to find that person in the United States. I think about the food, about the cassava leaves and the fried green bananas. I miss what I used to have, and what I used to want, who I thought I would become. But, at the same time, I don't.

12    Sometimes I am not sure whether home is behind me or in front of me. I am not so sure this longing is actually real. I might just be attaching it to those things that are familiar to me. Home might very well be a place that I have not yet discovered, that I have not yet created. Or it might not be a place at all. Home might be family, and nothing more. It might be the people who make me feel. The people who define and receive my emotions. The people who reciprocate,[15] who give me the most valuable gifts—acceptance, trust, laughter, comfort, love. In that case, Burundi is home and so is America.

[13] *cultural contrasts:* differences between cultures
[14] *mate:* a marriage partner
[15] *reciprocate:* to give or show in return

ACTIVITY 11    **Discussion** Discuss these questions with your classmates.

1.  Describe the frustration that Kambanda feels in paragraph 7.

2.  As you read more about her reactions in paragraphs 8, 9, and 10, do you think American telephones, washing machines, and eating habits make Kambanda feel negatively about America? Why or why not?

3.  Do you think she would leave America and go home if she did not have a commitment to school? Why or why not?

4.  Which sentence in paragraph 11 lets you know that she is not unhappy with her decision to come to the United States?

5.  Tell one way that Kambanda describes "home" in the final paragraph. Explain what you think she means.

**A. Group Activity** In Readings 1 and 2, Kambanda tells about aspects of daily life in the United States that she finds strange. In groups of 3–4, individually write two details of your own that you found strange when you came to the United States. Then share your details with your group. Do you or any of your group members find these details strange as well? Discuss your answers. Try to make a group list of at least three details that members of the group have in common.

**B.** Next, look at the following list of experiences that Kambanda writes about. Write each one in the category where it belongs. Experiences may fit into more than one category. You may not use all of the blanks.

Specific Experiences

using a washing machine

people rushing around without talking to each other

cars moving too fast

too many buttons to push

using a complicated telephone

too many lights

everyone eating fast food

too many escalators

| Fast Pace of Life in the United States | Impersonal Activities of Life in the United States | Complexity of Activities in the United States |
|---|---|---|
|  |  |  |
|  |  |  |
|  |  |  |
|  |  |  |

**C.** Now go back to the list of details that members of the group have in common. As a group, put these details in the above categories or make new categories if you need them. For example:

Topic: _Concern with time and being on time_

Detail: _Americans are always looking at their watches_

## Vocabulary

ACTIVITY 13 **Academic Words** Circle the letter of the definition that best matches the meaning of each boldface word.

1. It is **amazing** how busy Americans can be with the many activities in their lives.

   a. tiring    b. unbelievable    c. stressful

2. My cell phone is a telephone, a camera, an address book, a web browser, a video player, a calculator, and a calendar. Its **complexity** is unbelievable.

   a. sound quality    b. appearance    c. consisting of many parts or aspects

3. I am trying to **accomplish** all the things on my "to do" list before I go on vacation.

   a. make    b. pay for    c. complete

4. If you want to drive a car, you are **required** to have a driver's license.

   a. pushed    b. forced    c. trained

5. When I meet a lot of new people at a party, it is difficult for me to **recall** all their names.

   a. remember    b. guess    c. write down

6. In Burundi eating is a special part of each day so it never happens fast. People **attach** importance to this event.

   a. dine    b. remove    c. connect

7. I had so many **interruptions** at work today that it was impossible for me to finish my project.

   a. jobs to do    b. unexpected breaks    c. problems

8. He hardly ever sees his children. In fact, he has almost no **involvement** in their lives.

   a. participation    b. time    c. teaching

9. She is part of a **community** of women who do work with underprivileged children.

   a. a group of parents    b. a group of people with something in common

   c. a group of child specialists

10. It is often helpful to **display** a happy face even when you feel sad.

    a. give    b. show    c. make

11. Because you can sometimes guess the meanings of words from their context, it is not always necessary to **define** them.

    a. place in alphabetical order    b. display    c. give the meaning of

12. Most of the immigrants in California and Texas are of Hispanic origin. In these states, Hispanics make up the **majority** of the immigrants.

    a. nearly half    b. concept    c. more than half

## Composition Analysis

**Finding Levels of Generality** As you have seen, good writers use several levels of generality, ranging from very general to very specific, in order to make their points.

> **Level 1** (most general): Everyone in America seems in such a hurry that they eat only while doing something else at the same time.
>
> **Level 2** (next most general): They eat while they're driving, eat while they're talking on the phone, and even eat lunch at their desks while they're working.
>
> **Level 3** (most specific): The other day I even saw a woman eating lunch while she was walking down the street.

Writers do not always use all three levels to make a single point. However, they usually use at least two levels.

**ACTIVITY 14**

**A.** Choose statements from Reading 2 to fill in the missing levels.

1. **Level 1:** I had always thought of a telephone as a pretty basic unit.

    **Level 2:** Until I learned _____

2. **Level 1:** _____

    **Level 2:** You put your dirty clothes and some soap into a machine, close the lid, press a button, and within minutes, your clothes are done.

3. **Level 1:** _____

    **Level 2:** _____

    **Level 3:** Everyone ate at fast-food restaurants.

**B.** Put the following two statements in the correct order according to their level of specificity. Then add one more statement of your own that is at Level 3. *(Hint: Think about what you use a microwave for.)*

Using a microwave is one way to save time when cooking.

People are so busy that they don't have much time to cook.

4. **Level 1:** _____

   **Level 2:** _____

   **Level 3:** _____

## Making Connections

ACTIVITY 15 | Look at the progression of topics for Readings 1 and 2. Following each topic write as many details from the readings that support each topic as you can. The first one is done as an example. After you have completed the details, answer the questions that follow.

Progression of Topics in Reading 1

| sense of speed and complexity in the United States | → | feeling of guilt | → | determination to be the best |
|---|---|---|---|---|

Details

*people rushing around* _____ _____

_____ _____ _____

_____ _____ _____

_____ _____ _____

Progression of Topics in Reading 2

| kindness of host family | → | new aspects of daily life | → | feeling of having two homes |
|---|---|---|---|---|

Details

_____ _____ _____

_____ _____ _____

_____ _____ _____

_____ _____ _____

1. Why did Kambanda think she had to be the very best? _____

   _____

2. How did her first reaction to the United States contribute to this idea?

   _____

   _____

3. Why did Kambanda feel that she had two homes? _____

   _____

## Reading 3: Academic Reading

One very well-known refugee who eventually gained U. S. citizenship was the German physicist Albert Einstein. His work with Relativity and Quantum Mechanics in the early 1900s changed the course of scientific thinking forever after. In 1932, following several visits to the United States, he accepted a position at Princeton University. The idea was that Einstein would spend seven months a year in Germany and five months in the United States at Princeton. However, a month later the Nazis came to power in Germany. They believed Einstein was a public enemy because he was Jewish and a pacifist.[16] As a result, Einstein never again returned to Germany.

## Relativity

1    Suppose, as you are sitting in your car riding down the road, you are throwing a ball up and down in front of you. You would see the ball going straight up and down. However, someone standing by the roadside watching you drive by would see something completely different. He would see the ball moving forward as it goes up and down. Both of you would be correct, from your own points of view. What the ball is *really* doing depends on how you see it. The name for this concept is *relativity*. Relativity means what you observe and measure about an event depends on your

[16] *pacifist:* a person who is against war and violence

own point of view as well as the event itself. Observations are *relative* to the frame of reference, or viewpoint, of the observer.

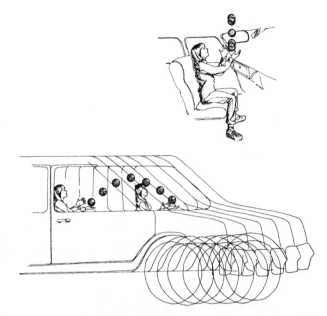

**Chart 1: Balls in the Air** The ball appears to move differently, depending on whether you view it from inside or outside the car.

2   Relativity also applies to larger events in the universe. For example, we can tell how fast our planet is moving only if we compare it to something else. Imagine a single planet in a completely empty universe. How fast is it moving? In what direction is it going? Unless we can compare it to some other object, those questions are meaningless.

3   Around 1900, a young German physicist named Albert Einstein wondered about relativity. How does it affect objects traveling at very high speeds? Light travels *very* fast: 300,000 kilometers per second in a vacuum.[17] Einstein wondered what light waves would look like to a person traveling at the speed of light. He realized one possible answer might be that the light would seem to be standing still (just as a person sitting next to you in a moving car seems to be sitting still).

4   However, Einstein also realized that answer didn't make sense. Light is made of waves, and waves must *move* to exist. So he decided to explore another possibility. He saw the speed of light must *always* be 300,000 kilometers per second, no matter how fast someone is moving when he or she observes it.

5   Einstein's law that the speed of light is always constant does not seem odd at first. But it doesn't fit our everyday, common sense view of nature. The velocities[18] of everything else in our world work by addition and subtraction. For example, suppose you are riding in a car at 50 miles per hour. You throw an apple core out the window at 10 miles per hour. The total velocity of the apple core must be 60 miles per hour.

6   Now imagine two stars, one moving toward the Earth at 100,000 kilometers per second and one moving away at the same rate. Both stars are producing light,

[17] *vacuum:* a space which is completely empty of matter
[18] *velocities:* speeds

which has a speed of 300,000 kilometers per second. If light acted like other things in our everyday world, we would expect the light from the first star to be moving toward us at 400,000 kilometers per second and the light from the other to be moving toward us at 200,000 kilometers per second. That would seem perfectly sensible.

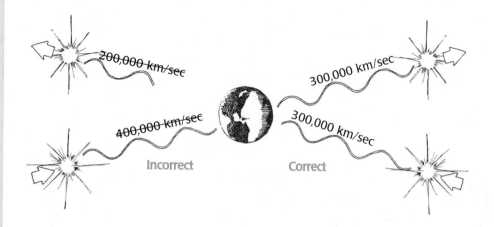

**Chart 2: Light Waves** The speed of light is always the same, no matter how fast the source of light may be moving either toward or away from us.

7     The trouble is, that isn't what happens. Scientists in the 1800s and early 1900s tried and tried to measure differences in the speed of light resulting from the motion of the Earth and stars. However, no matter how carefully scientists designed and carried out their experiments, light always measured 300,000 kilometers per second. Einstein understood this must be a basic rule of the universe.

8     The universal "speed limit" of light seems fairly simple. However, Einstein saw that if light always travels at a constant speed, the many other rules of the universe we considered "common sense" would have to change. Relativity predicted results that seem strange and very different from our everyday experiences. But every one of Einstein's predictions have proved true since his work was first published in 1905.

9     One of the most interesting ideas to come from Einstein's law of relativity is called *time dilation*. Time, as viewed by an outside observer, "slows down" as an object moves faster. Imagine a spaceship zooming past Earth at 200,000 kilometers per second. If we on Earth could somehow see the clocks on that ship, they would seem to be moving much too slowly. Imagine that the people on the spaceship could see Earth at the same time. They would see our planet flashing by at 200,000 kilometers per second. Everything on their ship would seem perfectly normal. But from their point of view, our clocks on Earth would seem much too slow!

10     As we can clearly see, relativity explains many odd realities that cannot be explained in any other way.

Excerpt from the book, *The Secrets of the Universe: Discovering the Universal Laws of Science*, by Paul Fleisher.

## Composition Analysis

**A Process Essay**  The purpose of a **process essay** is to explain the steps in a process in enough detail that the audience understands what they need to know. The level of detail depends on how much the audience already knows about the process and on how they need to apply the information. Sometimes the writer will use drawings or charts to illustrate ideas. This is particularly useful when describing a scientific process such as the Theory of Relativity.

In the Relativity essay, the explanation of the process begins with an everyday event supported by a drawing that provides an example of relativity. Second, it goes on to describe how relativity also applies to larger events in the universe. Third, it gives another example of how relativity explains these larger events. This is summarized below. Can you fill in the parts of the process?

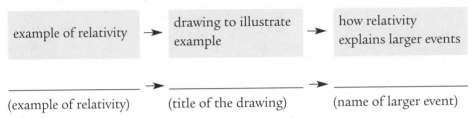

example of relativity → drawing to illustrate example → how relativity explains larger events

_____ → _____ → _____

(example of relativity)    (title of the drawing)    (name of larger event)

Notice that the order of these events is important. The process would not make sense if the order did not follow the above time line.

Let's consider one more example, the scientific concept of quantum mechanics, from the same author.

# Quantum Mechanics

Plank's law says the energy of light is directly proportional[19] to its frequency.[20] Frequency tells how fast the light wave vibrates[21] (vibrations per second). Light waves with higher frequencies vibrate more often in a given amount of time. Higher

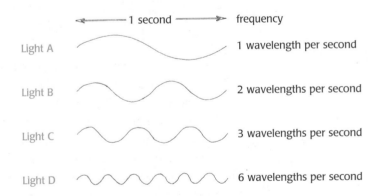

**Exhibit 1: Light Frequencies**  Light waves with higher frequencies have shorter wavelengths. If the waves are shorter, more wave crests will pass by a certain point in the same amount of time.

[19] *proportional:* directly related in size, degree, or other measurable characteristics
[20] *frequency:* the number of repetitions of a process per unit of time
[21] *vibrates:* moves up and down

frequency light also has shorter wavelengths than lower frequency light. That's because high frequency light vibrates more often in the same distance. The higher the frequency (and the smaller the wavelength) of light, the more energy it has.

Excerpt from the book, *The Secrets of the Universe: Discovering the Universal Laws of Science*, by Paul Fleisher.

In this example, the writer explains the characteristics of light waves and how they apply to quantum mechanics. In summary, the reader learns the following about light waves:

- Light waves with higher frequencies have more vibrations and shorter wavelengths.

- Light waves with higher frequencies have greater energy and intensity.

Exhibit 1 shows clearly the size of the wavelengths of four different kinds of light. It is easy to see how the frequencies and intensities of the different kinds of light compare with each other.

**ACTIVITY 16**

**A.** Answer the following questions using the information in the paragraph about quantum mechanics and Exhibit 1. Then write a reason to support your answer. The first one is done for you.

1. Does Light C have more energy than Light B?

   **Answer:** _Yes_

   **Reason:** _Light C has more wavelengths per second than Light B._

2. Does Light B have a higher intensity than Light C?

   **Answer:** _____

   **Reason:** _____

3. How many times greater is the frequency of Light C than the frequency of Light A?

   **Answer:** _____

   **Reason:** _____

4. How many more wavelengths per second does Light D have than Light A?

   **Answer:** _____

   **Reason:** _____

5. Which light has the greatest energy?

   **Answer:** _____

   **Reason:** _____

**B.** Use information from the paragraph and Exhibit 1 to write a supporting detail for each of the following statements. The first one is done for you.

1. The light with the least energy is Light A.

   **Supporting Detail:** *Light A has the fewest frequencies per second.*

2. Light D has a higher energy than Light C.

   **Supporting Detail:** _____

3. The frequency of Light B is twice as great as the frequency of Light A.

   **Supporting Detail:** _____

4. Statement: Light D has the greatest energy.

   **Supporting Detail:** _____

Now write your own statement and supporting detail about the paragraph and Exhibit 1.

5. _____

   **Supporting Detail:** _____

## Writing 2

**ACTIVITY 17**

To help you prepare for the writing assignment in Activity 18, choose a topic and discuss the questions with a partner who has chosen the same topic as you. Write answers to the questions in your own words. You do not need to agree with your partner as long as you can give reasons for your answers.

Topic 1

1. Tell your partner about a simple natural law that you understand, such as one from the list in Activity 18, Topic 1, below.

2. Tell how this law affects your everyday life.

Topic 2

1. Tell your partner about a simple process that you understand, such as one from the list in Activity 18, Topic 2, below.

2. Give some specific examples about how this process is useful or enjoyable in your everyday life.

Topic 3

1. Tell your partner about a simple labor-saving device that seems to really help people save time.

2. Is this device a good thing? Why or why not?

**Writing Assignment** Write a **process essay** about one of the following topics. Be sure to include in your paper all of the items in the checklist on page 184.

Topic 1

Choose a simple natural law of science that you are familiar with. Describe how the law works in everyday life. Draw a picture if you want to. Tell about what you can do in your life that is useful or enjoyable because of this law. If you use any unusual words, be sure to explain clearly what they mean.

**Possible Natural Laws:** gravity

boiling water

centrifugal force

*your choice*

Topic 2

Choose a simple process that you are familiar with. Describe the process and the result or purpose of the process. Tell why the process is useful or enjoyable to you. If you use any unusual words, be sure to explain clearly what they mean.

**Possible Processes:** operating a photocopier

using a digital camera

operating a pay telephone

cooking your favorite food

*your choice*

Topic 3

Choose a labor-saving device or action that you think provides an example of how "Americans have a way of wanting to accomplish as much as possible in as little time as possible." Explain it in detail. Then tell why you think it is positive or negative in life overall.

# Grammar

**Repetition of Key Words**

In Chapter 6 you learned about parallel structure, which refers to using the same pattern of words or phrases in a list. One kind of parallel structure makes use of the **repetition of specific key words** to create emphasis and cohesion.[22] This repetition draws attention and focus to important parts of the sentence (or sometimes sentences) it is in. Look at the following examples from Reading 2.

> Everything was rushed, was **too** this or **too** that, was always being pushed to the extreme.

In this sentence the repetition of the word *too* strengthens the idea that everything was *extreme* in some way.

> If someone is calling you, the phone rings, you answer it, and you talk. **No** interruptions, **no** complexities.

In the second sentence, the repetition of the word *no* emphasizes the simple steps in the first sentence.

> Until I learned that there was such a thing as call waiting. **And** then three-way calling. **And** call forwarding. **And** single telephone units with multiple lines.

In these sentences, the repetition of the word *and* emphasizes the great many features that telephones can have.

> I miss **what I used to** have, and **what I used to** want …

In this sentence, repetition of the phrase *what I used to* draws attention to the words *have* and *want*.

22 *cohesion:* the smooth flow and connection of words in a sentence or paragraph

---

**ACTIVITY 19**

Find another sentence in Reading 2 that uses **repetition of key words** to add emphasis and flow. Write the sentence here. *(Note: Sometimes the repetition of key words occurs in more than one sentence.)*

_____

_____

_____

**ACTIVITY 20**

Complete each of the following sentences using the given sentence parts and the repeated word. Use *and* or *or* before the final part. The first one is done as an example.

1. **Parts:** money down / payments for three months / credit problems

   **Repeated word:** no

   **Sentence:** If you buy a car from us, you will have _no money down, no_ _no payments for three months, and no credit problems._

2. **Parts:** a telephone with multiple lines / a washing machine to clean your clothes / a dryer to dry your clothes

   **Repeated word:** use

   **Sentence:** In America you can certainly save labor if you _____

   _____

   _____

3. **Parts:** doing other things / driving / being driven / sitting at their desks

   **Repeated word:** while

   **Sentence:** Americans like to eat _____

   _____

   _____

4. **Parts:** pick up the phone / dial a number / talk to someone

   **Repeated word:** you

   **Sentence:** Using a telephone should be a simple process; _____

   _____

   _____

5. **Parts:** cooking / eating / washing dishes / cleaning up the kitchen

   **Repeated word:** time

   **Sentence:** Americans always want to save time spent on food: _____

   _____

   _____

6. **Parts:** rules / exceptions to these rules

   **Repeated word:** many

   **Sentence:** English grammar is difficult to learn because it has _____

   _____

   _____

7. **Parts:** people / interruptions / exceptions

   **Repeated word:** any

   **Sentence:** I'm tired of speaking English. I'm going to my room. I don't want

   _____

   _____

Rewrite each of the following sentences to use repetition of key words. You may not use all of the words in the original sentence. The beginning of each sentence is there for you.

1. I have too many bills and I still have a debt. *(Hint: Repeat "too.")*

   I have too many bills and *too much debt.* _____

2. Home might not be a place at all, it might be family, or maybe home is people who make me feel, or there are the people who define and receive my emotions. *(Hint: Repeat "or it might be.")*

   Home might not be a place at all, it might be family _____

   _____

   _____

3. Home is the people that provide us with their acceptance, the trust we need, the laughter we want, and give us love. *(Hint: Repeat "their.")*

   Home is the people that provide us with their acceptance, _____

   _____

   _____

4. The idea behind Relativity is that what you observe about an event depends on your own point of view as much as what happens in the event itself. *(Hint: Repeat "depends on.")*

   The idea behind Relativity is that what you observe about an event depends on

   your own point of view as much as it _____

   _____

   _____

5. The Theory of Relativity cannot explain the behavior of an object that is without motion and does not have a direction. *(Hint: Repeat "without.")*

   The Theory of Relativity cannot explain the behavior of an object that is

   without motion _____

   _____

   _____

6. We can only tell what speed an object is moving and the direction it is going if we compare it to the speed and movement of another object. *(Hint: Repeat "what.")*

We can only tell what speed an object is moving and _____

_____

_____

7. Light frequency is the result of wave speed and the length of the waves. *(Hint: Repeat "wave.")*

Light frequency is the result of wave speed and _____

_____

_____

## Rewriting 2

ACTIVITY 22

**Peer Activity** Trade your paper from Activity 18 with another student. Read your partner's paper and underline the thesis statement. Then do one of the following:

1. If your partner wrote about Topic 1, write what the scientific law is. Then write what it does in everyday life. Write one detail. You do not need to write complete sentences.

2. If your partner wrote about Topic 2, write what the process is. Then write why it is useful or enjoyable to the writer. Write one detail. You do not need to write complete sentences.

3. If your partner wrote about Topic 3, write what the labor-saving device or action is. Then write why this is positive or negative to the writer. Write one detail. You do not need to write complete sentences.

Talk to your partner about what you found and help him or her make any necessary changes.

**On Your Own** Review your partner's notes, your partner's comments, and your teacher's feedback on the first draft of your composition. Use the Composition Evaluation Sheet (from Appendix 1) that your teacher returned to you to see specifically what you need to improve. Then consider the questions in the checklist below. Finally, rewrite your paper to make it clearer and more meaningful.

✓ CHECKLIST

**Content**

Do you identify the law, process, or device in your thesis statement?

Do you clearly explain your topic?

Do you use examples in your explanation?

**Organization**

Do you give details from at least two levels of generality?

Do you stick to the topic and avoid irrelevant sentences?

Does your conclusion connect to your thesis statement?

**Grammar**

Do you use adjective clauses correctly?

Do you use repetition of key words for emphasis?

## Internet Activities

For additional activities related to this chapter, go to elt.thomson.com/catalyst.

## Exploring the Topic

### ACTIVITY 1

**Discussion** We tend to think that others have the same values we have. However, different cultures often do not share the same values. But if we try to understand the basic beliefs behind the actions that express these values before we think of them as strange or unbelievable, we will all be better off.

In groups of 3–4, discuss the following ideas and questions. Then share your ideas with the class.

1. One example of a cultural value is "Competition brings out the best in an individual." Give another example.

2. Tell your group about one or two values that you live by. Where do you think these values came from?

3. Are there one or more common values in American society that you feel are in conflict with your own values? Explain one of these.

4. Do you think people can change their cultural values when they experience new ones that are different? Why or why not?

## PART 1

## Reading 1: Personal Experience Reading

Americans value individuality so highly that often they do not think of themselves as having values in common with members of their own culture. Consequently, they may not recognize that people from other cultures, with their own set of values, can find Americans difficult to understand. The values in this reading may help to explain American attitudes and behavior to the immigrant or foreign visitor. Can you predict one American value from your own experience that you think the reading will discuss?

As you read the article, think about how these values apply in situations you have experienced with Americans. You will use your thoughts later in this chapter.

## American Values for Better or Worse[1]

1   The very first European settlers, who came to North America more than four hundred years ago, came for religious and economic freedom and to escape from the control of kings and governments. With great difficulty and loss of life, they succeeded. In 1776, the United States of America declared their independence from England. Then in 1783, they won their independence. The new nation was built around several important values including individual freedom, self-reliance, productivity, equality, and free enterprise. These values have so deeply affected the culture of America that after hundreds of years they are still very much a part of everyday American life.

[1] *for better or worse:* with good and bad effect

### Individual Freedom and Self-Reliance[2]

2    Perhaps more than any other value, it is a spirit of freedom and self-reliance which has attracted millions of immigrants over the years. The idea that a person can take control of his or her own future without having rich parents or having a certain family background has made America "a land of opportunity" for many. Individuals are responsible for taking care of themselves. If they don't, they risk destroying their freedom. This is the way Americans think.

3    This individualism, however, does not come without a price. Although the rewards for self-reliance can be significant, individuals must decide their own direction and solve their own problems. If they succeed in the choices they make, they can take all the credit. But, if they fail, they must suffer the loss without much help. If they do get help from their families or the government or another organization, it should only be for a short time. Otherwise they may lose the respect of others and the freedom to do what they want. Americans believe that a person should be self-reliant. If they are not, they set a bad example.

4    This American concept of self-reliance runs against the thinking in many other cultures. In fact, English has many words beginning with "self," such as self-control, self-esteem, and self-respect, which are far less common in many other languages. However, the "self-made man or woman" is as much the ideal in America today as it was four hundred years ago.

### Productivity[3]

5    Americans are a people of action. In almost any situation, taking action, nearly any action, is better than inaction. From morning until night most Americans are active and busy. Any relaxation or "down time" is planned ahead, limited in time, and seen as a way to work harder and increase productivity afterwards. If rest goes on too long, the attitude will be that "sitting around doing nothing" is not the way to create a good life.

6    Along with these ideas about productivity comes an orientation[4] toward work. People tend to become "workaholics." Such people think constantly about their jobs, even during evenings and weekends. This, in turn, makes Americans very closely identified with their professions. One of the first questions an American will ask another when meeting for the first time is "Where do you work?" or "What do you do?"

7    In addition to work, another aspect of the intense desire to be productive is time orientation. Americans constantly make schedules and often follow them to the minute. They will cut off discussions, give up personal time with friends and family, and even skip lunch in order to be on time for the next appointment. They feel that such a tight timetable is the way to accomplish as much as possible.

8    A third result of a focus on productivity is an orientation to the future. The idea is that if you are to be productive, you must set goals. And in order to set goals, you must always be thinking ahead. And when you are always thinking ahead, you give up the present—again, connection with loved ones, or the pleasure of a happy moment. However, the rewards are plentiful. Americans are very good at

---

[2] *self-reliance:* depending on one's own ability
[3] *productivity:* the creation of something of value
[4] *orientation:* a direction of thought or feeling

completing short-term projects. They get the job done. Moreover, they are invited to all corners of the earth to plan and achieve the miracles[5] that their goal setting can produce.

9    However, such an attitude can be difficult to accept if you are from a culture that believes that only fate[6] is responsible for what is to come. Many people in the traditional Muslim world, for example, think that only fate is responsible for the future.

### Openness and Honesty

10    Americans have always preferred the direct approach. When it comes to telling people what they want or don't want, Americans generally waste no time. If you offer an American something to eat, he will most likely answer "yes" if he does and "no" if he doesn't. He is not likely to go through the polite formality of refusing several times before getting to the truth that he is hungry. Nor is he likely to accept food for your sake if he is not hungry.

11    Another argument that you can expect to avoid with an American is about who pays for a meal in a restaurant. First of all, it is very common that when people eat out together, each pays for her own meal, no matter who invited whom. However, if one person does offer to pay, an American will probably refuse once or twice out of politeness. Then, at that point, he will accept the offer saying, "Next time I'll buy," and the argument will end.

12    Americans are equally direct when it comes to saying "no." If an American says "no" to an invitation, it is not considered rude as long as he gives a reason. Sometimes these reasons are not completely honest. For example, he might say, "I can't meet you for dinner because I have to work late," when the real reason is that he wants to stay home and watch TV. However, this is still considered an acceptable answer. Conversely, in some other cultures saying "no" to an invitation is impolite. As a result, a person might say "no" indirectly by not showing up, which would be considered extremely rude in American culture.

13    Because of their direct and honest approach to life, Americans expect the same from others. They consider anything other than the most direct and open communication to be insincere. They distrust anyone who hints at the truth rather than coming out and saying it. Americans do not like to waste time or energy "beating around the bush".[7]

*(continued in Reading 2)*

[5] *miracle:* amazing or wonderful occurrence
[6] *fate:* the assumed force, principle, or power that makes events happen
[7] *beating around the bush:* approaching something indirectly

---

ACTIVITY 2    **Discussion** Discuss these questions with your classmates.

1.  What three kinds of freedom did the settlers want when they came to North America to build a new nation?

2.  Which of the values that the new nation was built around do you think best reflect this desire for freedom? Why do you think so?

3.  Why do you think the values of individual freedom and self-reliance are so appealing to immigrants from all over the world?

4. What are the three components of productivity? Do you think these components are positive? Why?

5. Give one example from the reading of how Americans are open and honest. How would you feel if an American behaved this way with you? Explain.

6. Give an example from your own experience of a time when an American expressed one of these values in some way. How did you feel about it?

## Vocabulary

ACTIVITY 3 **Academic Words** Write the letter of the correct definition for each **boldface** word in the blank.

_____ 1. He has an amazingly positive **attitude** about his job. He comes early and stays late nearly every day.

_____ 2. If you are a student of laziness and **inaction**, your

_____ 3. teacher will probably think you are **insincere** about learning.

_____ 4. It often takes an **intense** desire to succeed to make success happen.

_____ 5. When you learn a new language, it is nearly impossible to **eliminate** all your mistakes.

a. strong and well-focused
b. not believe in
c. recognition
d. very often
e. suggest indirectly
f. get rid of
g. way of thinking
h. associate
i. pride in oneself or self-respect
j. way of doing things
k. lack of activity
l. lacking in honesty

_____ 6. You will have many friends if you always try to give people the **credit** they deserve.

_____ 7. If you think about the things you do right every day, it can only help your **self-esteem**.

_____ 8. A value is a principle that people **identify** closely with.

_____ 9. If you **constantly** say one thing and do something else,

_____ 10. people are going to **distrust** you.

_____ 11. Children usually do not **hint** at what they want, they ask specifically.

_____ 12. There are times even for Americans when a more indirect **approach** is necessary to avoid seeming impolite.

# Composition Analysis

**Headings** Some articles and compositions use **headings** in addition to a title to contribute to points of focus. Headings also help to organize the information for easy reference and understanding.

In Reading 1, the title "American Values for Better or Worse" tells us that the reading will be about the relative good and bad aspects of the values that Americans live by. The headings then more specifically identify which American values are discussed. Next, each paragraph under the heading tells about one aspect of the value in the heading.

**Title:** American Values for Better or Worse

**Heading:** Individual Freedom and Self-Reliance

**Paragraph 2 Topic:** Freedom means a land of opportunity

**Paragraph 3 Topic:** Freedom means little or no help to deal with failure

**Paragraph 4 Topic:** Self-reliance goes against the attitude in many other cultures

**ACTIVITY 4**    Fill in the correct topics for each heading to show the organization of Reading 1.

1. **Heading:** Productivity

   **Paragraph 5 Topic:** _____

   **Paragraph 6 Topic:** _____

   **Paragraph 7 Topic:** _____

   **Paragraph 8 Topic:** _____

2. **Heading:** Openness and Honesty

   **Paragraph 10 Topic:** _____

   **Paragraph 11 Topic:** _____

   **Paragraph 12 Topic:** _____

   **Paragraph 13 Topic:** _____

# Writing 1

To help you prepare for the writing assignment in Activity 6, choose a topic and discuss the questions with a partner who has chosen the same topic as you. Write answers to the questions in your own words. You do not need to agree with your partner as long as you can give reasons for your answers.

### Topic 1

1. Tell your partner about a person you know who has a strong connection to one of the values in Activity 6, Topic 1, below.

2. How does this person express his or her connection to this value?

### Topic 2

1. Tell your partner about one of the values in Reading 1 that you find desirable.

2. Why do you feel positively about this value? Use examples from your own life to explain your answer.

### Topic 3

1. Tell your partner about one of the values in Reading 1 that you find undesirable.

2. Why do you feel negatively about this value? Use examples from your own life to explain your answer.

**ACTIVITY 6**

**Writing Assignment**  Write a composition about one of the following topics. Be sure you include in your paper all of the items in the checklist on page 194.

### Topic 1

Choose one of the values below. Then choose a person you know who has a strong connection to this value and write about the actions he or she takes in one day or one week that express this connection. Be sure to explain how the action shows this connection. You may also wish to include actions that this person does not take because the connection is so strong.

**Values:**   time orientation

work orientation

future orientation

### Topic 2

Choose one of the values from Reading 1 and give reasons why you think it is a positive value. Use examples from your own experience to support your reasons.

### Topic 3

Choose one of the values from Reading 1 and give reasons why you think it is a negative value. Use examples from your own experience to support your reasons.

# Grammar

**Transitions**

Writers use different words and phrases to show relationships between ideas. The **transitions** in the following sentences from Reading 1 are organized by meaning.

**Time Order:** shows the time an event happened in relation to other events

> **Then** in 1783 they won their independence.

**Great Importance:** shows that the importance of an idea comes before any others

> **First of all,** it is very common that when people eat out together, each pays for her own meal, no matter who invited whom.

**Emphasis, Cohesion, and Order:** draws attention to points that belong together

> **A third** result of a focus on productivity is an orientation to the future.

**Contrast:** sets two things in opposition

> If they succeed in the choices they make, they can take all the credit. **But,** if they fail, they must suffer the loss without much help.
> **Conversely,** in some other cultures saying "no" to an invitation is impolite.
> **However,** such an attitude can be difficult to accept if you are from a culture that believes that only fate is responsible for what is to come.

**Emphasis:** adds importance to something just mentioned

> **In fact,** English has many words beginning with "self," such as self-control, self-esteem, and self-respect, which are far less common in many other languages.

**Addition:** adds another item or detail to something just mentioned

> **Moreover,** they are invited to all corners of the earth to plan and achieve the miracles that their goal setting can produce.

**Example:** gives an example of something just mentioned

> **For example,** he might say, "I can't meet you for dinner because I have to work late,"...

Choose a word or phrase from the list to complete each sentence below. Do not add any other words. Some sentences may have more than one correct answer.

conversely   in fact   for example   moreover   but   then   however

1. I would be more than happy to go with you. _____ I have to finish my homework first.

2. Americans like to eat fast food. _____ the French like to spend several hours eating dinner.

3. Americans dress extremely informally. _____, they might go out to dinner in a nice restaurant wearing jeans.

4. First, check all your answers on the exam. _____ hand in your paper.

5. He is very smart. _____, he can speak six languages.

6. I enjoy hiking and cycling and being outdoors. _____, my sister would rather stay at home and read a book.

7. The English language contains more than 600,000 words. _____ it has thousands of idioms.

8. After working all day in my garden, I could hardly concentrate on studying.

   _____ I could hardly keep my eyes open.

**ACTIVITY 8**

Cross out each of the four **boldface** transition errors in the paragraph below. Then write a transition word from the list in Activity 7 in each blank that shows the correct relationship between ideas.

The values that Americans live by sometimes seem strange to immigrants and foreign visitors. (1) _____ **Then**, with some understanding of these values, it may be possible to avoid negative feelings. Americans believe most importantly that each person is in control of his or her own life. (2) _____ **For example**, they mistakenly believe that everyone else believes the same thing. (3) _____ **Conversely**, Americans so strongly hold this opinion that they may keep a little distance from other people to give them freedom to do exactly as they please. To Americans this may seem respectful. (4) _____ **In fact**, to people from other cultures, it may seem unfriendly or even rude.

# Rewriting 1

**Peer Activity** Trade your paper from Activity 6 with another student. Read your partner's paper and write at the top of the paper the value that the composition is about and what the point of view is. Ask your partner to underline one sentence that expresses each of the supporting points. Then check to see that they support the value and point of view you wrote at the top of the first page. Talk to your partner about what you found and help him or her make any necessary changes.

**On Your Own** Review your partner's notes, your partner's comments, and your teacher's feedback on the first draft of your composition. Use the Composition Evaluation Sheet (from Appendix 1) that your teacher returned to you to see specifically what you need to improve. Then consider the questions in the checklist below. Finally, rewrite your paper to make it clearer and more meaningful.

---

## ✔CHECKLIST

**Content**

Does your thesis statement present a point of view about the value that your composition is about?

Do you give adequate support for your point of view through explanation and examples?

Do you have any irrelevant sentences?

**Organization**

Do you identify in your thesis statement the American value your composition is about?

Does the topic sentence of each body paragraph support your thesis statement?

Do you give details from at least two levels of generality?

Does your conclusion successfully connect to your thesis statement and make an interesting point?

**Grammar**

Do you use transition words correctly?

---

## PART 2

## *Reading 2:* Extending the Topic Reading

Next to their values of individual freedom and self-reliance, Americans are perhaps best known for their values of equality, competition, and free enterprise. Most of the rest of the world, however, sees these values quite differently than Americans do.

As you read the article, think about how your home culture views these values. You will use your thoughts later in this chapter.

### *Equality*

14    Equality is, for Americans, one of their most cherished[8] values. This concept is so important for Americans that they have even given a religious basis for it. They say all people have been "created equally." Most Americans believe that God views all humans alike without regard to intelligence, physical condition, economic status, or rank.[9] This translates into the belief that all people have an equal opportunity to succeed in life.

15    This equality concept often makes Americans seem strange to foreigners because the majority of the world feels quite differently. To most of the rest of the world, rank and status and authority are extremely important. Class seems to give people in those societies a sense of security and certainty. People outside the United States consider it reassuring to know, from birth, who they are and where they fit into the complex system called "society."

16    Many highly-placed foreign visitors to the United States are insulted by the way waiters in restaurants, clerks in stores or hotels, taxi drivers, etc. treat them. Americans have a dislike of treating people of high position in a deferential[10] manner, and, conversely, often treat lower class people as if they are very important. If you are a foreigner in the United States, regardless of your status, you should be prepared to be considered "just like anybody else."

### *Competition and Free Enterprise*

17    Americans believe that competition brings out the best in any individual. They say that it forces each person to produce the very best that is humanly possible. Consequently, you will see competition encouraged in the American home and in the American classroom, even at the youngest age levels. Very young children, for instance, are encouraged to answer questions for which their classmates do not know the answers.

18    You may find the competitive value disagreeable, especially if you come from a society that promotes cooperation rather than competition among individuals. However, many U.S. Peace Corps volunteers teaching in developing nations[11] have found the lack of competitiveness in a classroom situation equally distressing. They

---

[8] *cherished:* held dear, or considered very important
[9] *rank:* a relative position in society
[10] *deferential:* yielding to the opinion, wishes, or judgment of another
[11] *nation:* a country

soon learned that what they had thought to be one of the universal human characteristics represents only an American (or Western) value.

19    Americans, because they value competition so strongly, have created an economic system to go with it—free enterprise. Americans feel very strongly that a highly competitive economy will bring out the best in its people and that such a society will progress most rapidly. If you look for it, you will see evidence in all areas, as diverse as medicine, the arts, education, and sports, that free enterprise is the approach most often preferred in America.

### Informality

20    If you come from a more formal society, you will likely find Americans to be extremely informal. You may even feel they are disrespectful of those in authority. Americans are one of the most informal and casual people in the world. One example of this informality is the way American bosses often urge their employees to call them by their first names and even feel uncomfortable if they are called by the title "Mr." or "Ms."

21    Dress is another area where American informality will be most noticeable, perhaps even shocking. You can go to a symphony performance, for example, in any large American city and find some people in the audience dressed in blue jeans, short-sleeved shirts, and without ties.

22    Informality is also apparent in Americans' greetings. The more formal "How are you?" has largely been replaced with an informal "Hi." This is used almost as often with one's superior as with one's best friend.

23    If you are a highly placed official in your own country, you will probably find such informality to be very unsettling. Americans, on the other hand, consider such informality a compliment, as if to say, "We're together as one. We're on the same level." Certainly it is not intended as a personal insult,[12] and you should not take it as such.

---

[12] *insult:* a rude action or comment directed at a person

---

ACTIVITY 11    **Discussion** Discuss these questions with your classmates.

1. What does it mean that the value of equality has a religious basis?

2. How does most of the rest of the world see the concept of equality?

3. What is a value that could be considered the opposite of competition? Which of these two opposite values do you prefer? Why?

4. Based on the values discussed in Readings 1 and 2, why do you think Americans are so informal?

5. Give an example from your own experience of how Americans are informal.

**Group Activity** In groups of 3–4, discuss the situations below. In each of the situations, an immigrant and an American have some kind of interaction in which the immigrant experiences confusion, frustration, embarrassment, or anger because of a conflict in values. Next decide which value or values that you have studied are present in the situation. Then decide what you think the immigrant should understand about American values that would help ease his or her negative feelings about the situation. The first one is done as an example.

1. **Situation:** You are at a restaurant with your mother. An American classmate of yours comes in and you greet each other. Then you introduce your mother by saying, "This is my mother Bertha Martinez." Your classmate smiles and says, "So nice to meet you, Bertha." You are embarrassed for your mother about what your classmate just said.

   **Value(s):** _Informality, Equality_

   **What needs to be understood:** _Americans often address people by their first names regardless of age and even if they don't know them well._

2. **Situation:** You are an immigrant who knows a few of your co-workers a little bit and they seem quite friendly. You think you would like to know them better so you suggest to them that you get together for lunch once a week. They say this is a good idea, but when you try to find a day one of them says she usually swims at lunch time. Another says he usually eats at his desk so he can leave work in time to watch his kids' baseball games. Another says she can't leave the phone during lunch hour because customers often call at that time. You feel a little frustrated about this and wonder if maybe they don't really like you very much.

   **Value(s):** _____

   **What needs to be understood:** _____

   _____

3. **Situation:** You are a student new to the United States. You have been invited to spend the day with an American family. You meet them at 10:00 in the morning and immediately go to an arts and crafts festival.[13] Then you have lunch at one of their favorite seafood restaurants. After lunch you enjoy a walk in the park and a visit to a museum. Dinner is in another restaurant that is quite crowded and noisy so it is difficult to have a conversation. At the end of the day you are very happy and thankful for everything your hosts have done for you. But you are also very tired and you don't really feel you have gotten to

[13] *festival:* an outdoor celebration where artists display their work

know this family. You wonder, why didn't we just stay home and talk together and then go out for a little while if we felt like it?

**Value(s):** _____

**What needs to be understood:** _____

_____

4. **Situation:** You are an immigrant invited out to dinner in a restaurant with an American family. As soon as you all arrive, the American children jump out of the car and run into the restaurant to find a table for everyone. They order their own food from the menu without discussing their choices with their parents. They do not finish their meals because they have ordered more food than they can eat. Their parents say nothing about their behavior. Because the children are done before the rest of you, they leave the table telling their parents they want to play video games in a far corner of the restaurant. Their parents agree to this. You are quite surprised and confused by the independence of the children. Do these parents not know how to discipline their children, do they just not care, or are they trying to teach them to take care of themselves? You are not sure.

**Value(s):** _____

**What needs to be understood:** _____

_____

Make up a situation from your own personal experience.

5. **Situation:** _____

_____

_____

_____

**Value(s):** _____

**What needs to be understood:** _____

_____

# Vocabulary

**Academic Words** Choose the word that is similar in meaning to the boldface word or words.

1. Police officers have the **power** to enforce the law.

   a. title    b. authority    c. credit

2. One form of financial **safety** is having money in the bank.

   a. security    b. competition    c. performance

3. It is **encouraging** when you make a decision and someone tells you you did the right thing.

   a. reassuring    b. distressing    c. universal

4. Exercise **contributes to** good health.

   a. treats    b. promotes    c. prefers

5. There was **an outward sign** that someone had been in our house while we were gone.

   a. cooperation    b. evidence    c. encouragement

6. He has many interests, as **different** as skateboarding and classical music.

   a. shocking    b. diverse    c. opposite

7. It was **clear** from the time he spends with his children that he loves them very much.

   a. informal    b. secure    c. apparent

8. In American classrooms it is common that students **try to be the best** in the class.

   a. are competitive    b. are uncomfortable    c. are encouraging

9. In America it is **an expression of praise** to be called by your first name.

   a. an urge    b. an attitude    c. a compliment

10. It is **painful** for an immigrant to be in a culture where new values are in conflict with his old values.

    a. insulting    b. distressing    c. reassuring

Fill in the missing word forms in the chart below. Use your dictionary to check word forms you don't know. An X means that there is no common word form for a certain part of speech. (See Word Form Suffixes in Appendix 5 on page 219.)

| Noun | Verb | Adjective | Adverb |
|---|---|---|---|
| authority | | authorized, authoritative | |
| | secure | | |
| promotion | | | |
| | | complimentary | X |
| | intend | | |
| cooperation | | | cooperatively |
| reassurance | | reassuring | |
| | X | | evidently |
| competitiveness, competition | | | competitively |
| | | distressing | |

## Composition Analysis

**Using "you" to Connect to the Reader** When attempting to connect the reader closely to the reading, the writer will sometimes address the reader as "**you**." This is a personal, and therefore informal, approach so it is not appropriate for formal writing such as serious academic essays. However, it puts the reader right in the center of the situation, which can at times be useful. Look at the following examples from Reading 2:

> If **you** are a foreigner in the United States, regardless of your status, **you** should be prepared to be considered "just like anybody else."

> **You** may find the competitive value disagreeable, especially if **you** come from a society that promotes cooperation rather than competition among individuals.

> If **you** come from a more formal society, **you** will likely find Americans to be extremely informal. **You** may even feel they are disrespectful of those in authority.

Each of these sentences encourages the reader to put herself in the situation in the *if* subordinate clause and then to read on to find out what the result will be.

Rewrite each of the following sentences using an *if* subordinate clause and *you*. The first one is done for you.

1. Highly placed officials from other countries often find American informality unsettling.

   **Rewrite:** _If **you** are a highly placed official from another country,_

   _**you** will often find American informality unsettling._

2. There is evidence in many areas, such as medicine, the arts, education, and sports, that free enterprise is the approach Americans prefer.

   **Rewrite:** _____

   _____

3. People from other countries notice that Americans don't like to "sit around and waste time."

   **Rewrite:** _____

   _____

4. Most likely an American teacher called by his first name will not be offended.

   **Rewrite:** _____

   _____

5. Someone from a society that promotes cooperation will notice that competition is often encouraged in American homes and classrooms.

   **Rewrite:** _____

   _____

6. It is clear to foreign visitors that rank, status, and authority are not important to Americans.

   **Rewrite:** _____

   _____

# Making Connections

Look at the headings from Readings 1 and 2.

| Reading 1 | Reading 2 |
|---|---|
| Individual Freedom and Self-Reliance | Equality |
| Productivity | Competition and Free Enterprise |
| Openness and Honesty | Informality |

Think about what you have learned in Readings 1 and 2 about these American values. For each value in Reading 1, write the value from Reading 2 that you think most closely connects to it. Then give a reason for your answer. You may not use all of the values from Reading 2. You may use the same value more than once.

1. Hard Work  *Material Wealth*

   **Reason:** *People work hard to have material wealth.*

2. Individual Freedom and Self-Reliance _____

   **Reason:** _____

   _____

3. Productivity _____

   **Reason:** _____

   _____

4. Openness and Honesty _____

   **Reason:** _____

   _____

# Hybrid-Electric Vehicles

1    In addition to such basic American values as individual freedom and self-reliance, productivity, and openness and honesty, we are also seeing an increased desire to preserve the environment. As this idea mixes in the minds and hearts of Americans with their love of the automobile, the result is the enormous popularity of hybrid-electric vehicles. These vehicles, which combine gasoline power with electric power, do their part to reduce American dependence on oil and reduce harmful emissions.[14]

### What Is a Hybrid-Electric Vehicle?

2    It is no accident that the most fuel-efficient vehicles available today are hybrid-electric vehicles (HEVs). Hybrids combine a small combustion engine with an electric motor and battery. The two technologies together reduce fuel consumption and emissions without giving up performance or driving range.[15] This makes them an excellent choice for the environmentally-conscious American.

### How Do Hybrids Get Such Great Gas Mileage?

3    HEVs are powered by an internal combustion engine, just like other vehicles on the road. However, they also turn energy normally wasted during coasting[16] and braking into electricity. This electricity is stored in a battery until needed by the electric motor. The electric motor assists the engine when the vehicle is accelerating or hill climbing and also takes over in low-speed driving conditions. This allows a smaller, more efficient engine to be used. Most HEVs also automatically shut off the engine when the vehicle comes to a stop and restart it when the driver presses the accelerator.[17]

4    Unlike all-electric vehicles, HEVs do not need to be plugged into an external source of electricity to be recharged; conventional gasoline and "regenerative braking"[18] provide all the energy the vehicle needs.

### How Do They Affect Air Pollution and Global Warming?

5    Hybrids can reduce smog pollution by ninety percent or more compared with the cleanest conventional vehicles on the road today. Global-warming pollutants

---

[14] *emissions:* waste products discharged into the air by the burning of gasoline
[15] *driving range:* the distance a vehicle can go on one tank of gas
[16] *coasting:* rolling down hill
[17] *accelerator:* a pedal used to supply a car engine with gas
[18] *regenerative braking:* when the vehicle is slowing down it creates and captures power for use later

can be cut by a third to a half and perhaps even more in the future. Hybrids will, however, never be true zero-emission vehicles because of their internal-combustion engines.

### What About Range and Performance?

6    By combining gasoline with electric power, hybrids will have greater range than traditional combustion engines. The actual range depends on the size of the gas tank. Some HEVs can go as much as 700 miles on a single tank of gas. For the driver, hybrids offer similar or better performance compared with conventional vehicles. They're fun, they're smooth, and they're responsive.

### What About Cost?

7    The purchase price of an HEV may be a few thousand dollars more than a similar conventional vehicle. However, when all the costs over the life of the vehicle are included, the price is very competitive. First of all, the fuel cost of a hybrid will be far less. Second, federal tax deductions as well as state tax credits may be available.

8    Therefore, in terms of fuel efficiency, pollution control, and cost, an HEV provides an attractive alternative to a conventional gasoline vehicle. Owners can drive them without losing the range and performance they are used to. Even better, owners can be satisfied knowing that they are making a positive contribution to the environment.

## Composition Analysis

**An Evaluation Essay**   The purpose of an **evaluation essay** is to lead the reader through an analysis of a topic in order to convince her of a particular point of view. One way that a writer may try to do this is by asking questions that he thinks will be in the reader's mind.

Look at the headings in Reading 3. What is the structure of all of the headings? What purpose do all of the headings have in common?

As you may have guessed, all of the headings are questions. The purpose of the questions is to address what the writer predicts the reader will wonder about.

By addressing questions that the writer thinks the reader will wonder about, what is the writer trying to do? What is the writer's point of view? What is the writer trying to persuade the reader of?

You may have answered that the writer is trying to draw the reader in so that he can persuade the reader of his own point of view that hybrids are good cars to own.

Imagine that you want to convince your reader of the benefits of American productivity as a means of achieving goals. Write questions for Headings 2, 3, and 4 that you would use to write a composition to persuade your reader. Headings 1 and 5 are done for you as examples. Then write a conclusion.

**Heading 1:** _Why are Americans so productive?_

**Heading 2:** _____

**Heading 3:** _____

**Heading 4:** _____

**Heading 5:** _How will American productivity affect the future?_

**Conclusion:** _____

_____

_____

# Writing 2

ACTIVITY 18

To help you prepare for the writing assignment in Activity 19, choose a topic and discuss the questions with a partner who has chosen the same topic as you. Write answers to the questions in your own words. You do not need to agree with your partner as long as you can give reasons for your answers.

Topic 1

1. Which value in Reading 2 do you find the most positive?

2. What is the biggest problem that this value causes for some people?

Topic 2

1. Which value in Reading 2 do you find the most negative?

2. What is one positive aspect of this value?

Topic 3

1. Tell your partner which of the items in the "Your Situation" list in Activity 19, Topic 3, are the very most important to you. Give your reasons.

2. Tell your partner which features in the two "Vehicle Features" lists in Activity 19, Topic 3, best meet your needs.

3. Did you find more of these features in the HEV list or in the SUV list?

**Writing Assignment** Write an **evaluation essay** about one of the following topics. Be sure to include in your paper all of the items in the checklist on page 210.

### Topic 1

Choose one of the values in Reading 2 that you think is positive. Write about what you think is the strongest objection to this value. Explain why you still think it is positive. Give reasons from your own experience or from what you have read to support your point.

### Topic 2

Choose one of the values in Reading 2 that you think is negative. Write about what you think is the most positive aspect of this value. Explain why you think it is positive. Give reasons from your own experience or from what you have read to support your point.

### Topic 3

You are in the market for a new car. You have decided you will buy either an HEV or SUV (Sport Utility Vehicle). Look at "Your Situation" and the lists of "Vehicle Features" below. Then evaluate and choose the vehicle that seems best and write a composition giving three reasons for your choice.

**Your Situation**

- You are a parent who needs room for your five-person family.
- You are concerned about the environment and air pollution.
- You are concerned about the high cost of gas.
- You are concerned about the cost of yearly service.
- You usually drive in snow in the mountains a few times each winter when you go skiing.
- You sometimes need to carry some boxes and equipment to work.

**Vehicle Features**

| HEV Features | SUV Features |
|---|---|
| Gets more than 50 miles per gallon of gas | Gets 18–22 miles per gallon of gas |
| Can carry five passengers with little baggage | Can carry five passengers with much baggage |
| Yearly cost of service—about $400 | Yearly cost of service—about $550 |
| Front wheel 2-wheel drive | 4-wheel drive—good for snow driving |
| 40 cubic feet of cargo space with seats down | 60 cubic feet of cargo space with seats down |

# Grammar

**Verb Tense Consistency**

Clear writing requires **verb tense consistency**. This means that writers maintain one primary verb tense, usually the simple present or the simple past, to show the time when related events take place. However, writers at times indicate changes in the time of events by changing tenses. Changes in verb tense, if consistent, help readers understand the time relationships between the events. Look at the following examples from Reading 2.

> You may **find** the competitive value disagreeable, especially if you come from a society that promotes cooperation rather than competition among individuals. However, many U.S. Peace Corps volunteers teaching in developing nations **have found** the lack of competitiveness in a classroom situation equally distressing. They soon **learned** that what they had thought to be one of the universal human characteristics represents only an American (or Western) value.

The first and second sentences are in the present time (present and present perfect tenses). They tell the reader that it is possible that she finds the competitive value disagreeable and that Peace Corps volunteers have found the lack of it distressing. The third sentence then shifts to past time (simple past tense) to say that Peace Corps volunteers learned when they were teaching that competition is not a universal value.

> Americans, because they **value** competition so strongly, **have created** an economic system to go with it—free enterprise. Americans **feel** very strongly that a highly competitive economy **will bring** out the best in its people and that such a society will progress rapidly.

The first sentence is in the present time (present and present perfect tenses). It tells the reader that currently Americans strongly value competition and they have for some time. The second sentence then shifts to future time to say that Americans believe that the highly competitive free enterprise system is the future of America.

Inconsistent changes in tense (time) can cause confusion. Do not shift from one tense (time) to another if the time frame for each action is the same.

*Correct:* As the idea of preserving the environment **mixes** in the minds and hearts of Americans with their love of the automobile, the result **is** the enormous popularity of hybrid electric vehicles.

*Incorrect:* As the idea of preserving the environment **mixes** in the minds and hearts of Americans with their love of the automobile, the result **was** the enormous popularity of hybrid electric vehicles.

Fill each blank with the correct form of the verb in parentheses.

1. Many people think Americans are rude because they treat all people equally, but the truth is they just (**want**) _____ to be "one" with everyone.

2. The idea of equality often makes Americans seem strange to foreigners because the majority of the world (**feel**) _____ quite differently.

3. Some Americans are so casual in the way they dress that if they are going to go to a symphony performance, they (**wear**) _____ jeans.

4. Americans believe that competition (**bring**) _____ out the best in an individual because it makes him (**strive**) _____ to do better than anyone else.

5. Electric vehicles (**be**) _____ around for many years, but hybrid vehicles (**be**) _____ relatively new.

6. In societies where class exists, it seems to give people a sense that they know where they (**fit**) _____ into the complex system called "society."

7. Her boss urged her to call him by his first name, but she always (**feel**) _____ uncomfortable doing so. She can't get used to it.

8. Hybrid vehicles greatly reduce air pollution, but they never (**be**) _____ completely emission free because they do burn gas.

Correct the ten inconsistent verb tense errors in the following paragraph.

The behaviors of people in a particular culture only make sense if you **looked** at them with an understanding of their cultural values. For example, if you ask an American for directions to a particular address, it **was** not likely that he **walks** a couple of city blocks to show you the location personally. It is far more likely that he **explains** in great detail how you can find the place on your own. This may seem confusing and unfriendly to you if you **experience** something different in your own country in the past. However, if you **considering** the American attitude of self-reliance, you **understand** that the American might be **try** hard to help you remain independent. It **will** also **be** possible that his sense of future orientation is making him feel that he **teaches** you to find other locations in the future.

# Rewriting 2

**ACTIVITY 22**  **Peer Activity** Trade your paper from Activity 19 with another student. Read your partner's paper. Then, with your partner, make an outline of the composition. When you are finished, check to see that the composition and the outline contain the same information. Next check to see that the levels of specificity are organized correctly in the outline. Finally, help your partner make any necessary changes to his or her composition based on the outline you made together.

**ACTIVITY 23**  **On Your Own** Review your partner's notes, your partner's comments, and your teacher's feedback on the first draft of your composition. Use the Composition Evaluation Sheet (from Appendix 1) that your teacher returned to you to see specifically what you need to improve. Then consider the questions in the checklist below. Finally, rewrite your paper to make it clearer and more meaningful.

## ✓CHECKLIST

### Content

For Topics 1 and 2, does your thesis statement give your point of view about the value you are writing about?

For Topic 3, does it give your point of view about your choice of vehicles?

Do you have any irrelevant sentences?

For Topics 1 and 2, does your conclusion make an interesting point about one American value?

For Topic 3, does your conclusion summarize the reasons for your choice?

### Organization

For Topics 1 and 2, does your thesis statement identify the value you are writing about?

For Topic 3, does your thesis statement identify your choice of vehicles?

Do all of your reasons connect to the point they should support?

Do your reasons include at least two levels of generality?

Does your conclusion connect to your thesis statement?

### Grammar

Do you use transition words and phrases correctly?

Do you use verb tenses consistently?

# Internet Activities

For additional activities related to this chapter, go to elt.thomson.com/catalyst.

## *Composition Evaluation Sheet*

| | Excellent or Very Good | OK | Needs Improvement |
|---|---|---|---|
| **Content and Ideas** | | | |
| Addresses the assignment correctly | 4–5 | 2–3 | 0–1 |
| Shows the writer has an understanding of the topic | 4–5 | 2–3 | 0–1 |
| Presents an interesting and believable point of view | 4–5 | 2–3 | 0–1 |
| Sentences are all relevant to the topic | 4–5 | 2–3 | 0–1 |
| **Introduction** | | | |
| Introduces the topic | 4–5 | 2–3 | 0–1 |
| Contains a clear topic with a controlling idea | 4–5 | 2–3 | 0–1 |
| Shows how the writer will organize the composition | 4–5 | 2–3 | 0–1 |
| Moves from general to specific | 4–5 | 2–3 | 0–1 |
| **Body Paragraphs** | | | |
| Has one body paragraph for each main point | 4–5 | 2–3 | 0–1 |
| Has clear topic sentences with controlling ideas | 4–5 | 2–3 | 0–1 |
| Has relevant details to support each topic sentence | 4–5 | 2–3 | 0–1 |
| Each topic sentence supports the thesis statement | 4–5 | 2–3 | 0–1 |
| **Conclusion** | | | |
| Restates or summarizes the main idea of the thesis statement | 4–5 | 2–3 | 0–1 |
| Makes a prediction, offers a suggestion, or gives an opinion | 4–5 | 2–3 | 0–1 |
| **Support** | | | |
| Detail sentences support each main point | 4–5 | 2–3 | 0–1 |
| Detail sentences are all relevant to the points they support | 4–5 | 2–3 | 0–1 |
| Main points have similar amounts of detail to support them | 4–5 | 2–3 | 0–1 |
| **Organization** | | | |
| Has a clear beginning, middle, and end | 4–5 | 2–3 | 0–1 |
| Main points follow logical order | 4–5 | 2–3 | 0–1 |
| Has transitions between ideas | 4–5 | 2–3 | 0–1 |
| **Sentence Structure and Punctuation** | | | |
| Has few grammatical errors | 4–5 | 2–3 | 0–1 |
| Errors do not interfere with meaning | 4–5 | 2–3 | 0–1 |
| Uses correct word order | 4–5 | 2–3 | 0–1 |
| Uses correct punctuation, capitalization, and spelling | 4–5 | 2–3 | 0–1 |
| Uses a variety of simple, compound, and complex sentences | 4–5 | 2–3 | 0–1 |

Total Score _____

## Generating Ideas for Writing Topics

All of the writing topics in this book are directly or indirectly related to the readings. Therefore, a good place to start is to review your answers to the Discussion questions that follow the reading that the topic is based on. After reviewing them, do the following:

1. Write the topic or key words of the topic on a piece of paper.

2. Below the topic, write as many ideas that come to mind about the topic as you can. Do not think about grammar or spelling. Do not leave out any ideas or try to organize as you write. Try to keep your pen moving for several minutes (at least) so you keep your ideas flowing.

3. After you have as many ideas as you can think of, go back and circle the ideas that you might want to use in your composition.

4. Try to put these ideas into categories according to something they have in common. For example:

   *Category:* My Goals for the Next Five Years
   *Ideas:* complete my college degree
   get a job in computer science
   gain U.S. citizenship

5. Select the categories that seem the most interesting and relevant to the topic. It may be that one category will give you enough points for your composition. Or you may want to use two or three categories: one for each major point.

6. Organize your categories (if you have more than one) into a logical order.

7. Organize the points within your category (or within each category) into a logical order.

8. Make an outline of your composition based on the organization of your ideas.

9. Read the topic assignment one more time and make sure that all of your ideas fit with the topic. Change or eliminate any that are not relevant to the topic.

10. Write a topic sentence or thesis statement that gives your point of view and tells how you will handle the topic.

## Summary of Transition and Connection Words

| Transitions | Meaning | Transition | Chapter |
|---|---|---|---|
| | at a certain point in time | at that moment | 3 |
| | at that time | just then | 3 |
| | going on at the present | by this time | 3 |
| | addition | in addition | 3 |
| | | moreover | 8 |
| | too bad | unfortunately | 3 |
| | coming unexpectedly | suddenly | 3 |
| | coming without warning | all at once | 3 |
| | at the end | at last | 3 |
| | in the end | finally | 3 |
| | next | then | 3 |
| | after a time | later | 3 |
| | contrast | however | 4, 8 |
| | | on the one hand | 4 |
| | | on the other hand | 4 |
| | | in contrast | 4 |
| | | conversely | 4, 8 |
| | comparison | likewise | 4 |
| | | similarly | 4 |
| | | in the same way | 4 |
| | | like | 4 |
| | | similar to | 4 |
| | | just like | 4 |
| | | (be) similar to | 4 |
| | | (be) the same as | 4 |
| | time order | then | 8 |
| | great importance | first of all | 8 |

| Transitions, *continued* | Meaning | Transition | Chapter |
|---|---|---|---|
| | emphasis, cohesion, and order | first | 8 |
| | | second | 8 |
| | | third | 8 |
| | | a first/second/third | 8 |
| | emphasis | in fact | 8 |
| | example | for example | 8 |

| Connecting Prepositions | Purpose | Connector | Chapter |
|---|---|---|---|
| | following | after | 3 |
| | because of | based on | 3 |
| | addition | besides | 3 |

| Coordinators | Purpose | Coordinator | Chapter |
|---|---|---|---|
| | contrast | but | 4, 8 |
| | | yet | 4 |
| | comparison | and | 4 |
| | | and so | 4 |
| | | also | 4 |

| Subordinators | Purpose | Subordinator | Chapter |
|---|---|---|---|
| | contrast | though | 4 |
| | | although | 4 |
| | | even though | 4 |
| | | while | 4 |
| | comparison | just as | 4 |

## *Punctuation Summary*

**Subordinators** connect a dependent clause and an independent clause in one sentence. Use a comma after the dependent clause when it comes before the independent clause.

> **Although** I was very tired, I stayed up to finish my homework.

Do not use a comma when the independent clause comes before the dependent clause.

> I stayed up to finish my homework **although** I was very tired.

**Coordinators** connect two independent clauses in one sentence. Use a comma after the first clause.

> I wanted to call my mother, **but** I ran out of time.

**Transition Words** connect two independent clauses or two sentences. For two independent clauses, use a semicolon after the first clause and a comma after the transition word.

> Hiro wants his mother to come and live with them; **however**, Hanna is against it.

For two sentences, use a period after the first sentence and a comma after the transition word in the second sentence.

> He is loud and talkative. **By contrast**, his brother is quiet and shy.

## Word Form Suffixes

| Nouns | Verbs | Adjectives | Adverbs |
|---|---|---|---|
| -ance/-ence | -ate | -ant | -ly |
| -ee | -ize | -al | |
| -ment | -en | -ive | |
| -er/-or | | -ly | |
| -sion/-tion | | -able/-ible | |
| -ness | | -ic | |
| | | -ous | |

## Skills Index

## Speaking

## Topics

## Vocabulary

## Writing

## Chapter 1

Reading 1, pp. 2–4: Excerpt from Danna Harman, "The Struggle to Support Faraway Families." This article first appeared in *The Christian Science Monitor* on January 14, 2004, and is reproduced with permission. Copyright © 2004 *The Christian Science Monitor* (www.csmonitor.com). All rights reserved.

Reading 2, pp. 12–13: From Jeremy Scott-Joynt, "The Remittance Lifeline," BBC News, 3/18/04. Adapted by permission.

Reading 3, pp. 18–20: Excerpt from Andres Maldonado and Alejandra Robledo, "Sending Money Back Home," *The McKinsey Quarterly 2002*, Number 4. Reprinted by permission.

## Chapter 2

Reading 2, pp. 39–41: Him Mark Lai, et al., excerpts from *Island: Poetry and History of Chinese Immigrants on Angel Island, 1910–1940* (Seattle: University of Washington Press, 1980), pp. 72, 75, 116.

Reading 3, pp. 47–48: From *Five Views: A History of Japaneses Americans in California*, www.cr.nps.gov.

## Chapter 3

Readings 1 and 2, pp. 54–56, 64–66: Excerpts from Lynne Cox, "The Bering Strait Swim," from *Swimming to Antarctica* (Alfred Knopf, 2004). Used by the permission of Alfred A. Knopf, a division of Random House, Inc.

## Chapter 4

Reading 2, pp. 92–93: From *Video Letter from Japan: My Family, 1988*, pp. 36–37, www.askasia.org.

Reading 3, pp. 101–102: From "Wedding Traditions in Pakistan and Wedding Traditions in Sudan," www.worldweddingtraditions.com.

## Chapter 5

Reading 1, pp. 110–112: From Helen Zia, *Asian American Dreams* (Farrar, Straus & Giroux, 2000). Reprinted by permission.

Reading 2, pp. 120–121: Excerpt from Jeanne Park, "Eggs, Twinkies, and Ethnic Stereotypes," © 1990, *The New York Times*. Reprinted by permission.

Reading 3, pp. 125–126: Kimberly Hohman, "Model Minority," from racerelations.about.com. Reprinted by permission of the author.

## Chapter 6

Reading 1, pp. 134–135: From William Branigin, "Immigrants Question Idea of Assimilation," © 1998, *The Washington Post*. Excerpted and adapted with permission.

Reading 2, pp. 143–144: "Choosing Your Battle," from *Serving in Silence* by Margarethe Cammermeyer, © 1994 by Margarethe Cammermeyer. Used by permission of Viking Penguin, a division of Penguin Group (USA) Inc.

Reading 3, pp. 148–149: Excerpt from Peter D. Salins, *Assimilation, American Style*. Reprinted by permission of Basic Books, a member of Perseus Books Group.

## Chapter 7

Readings 1 and 2, pp. 158–159, 167–168: Excerpts from Nola Kambanda, "My New World Journey," from *Becoming American,* Meri Nana-Ama Danquah, ed. (Hyperion, 2000). Reprinted by permission of Nola Kambanda and The Watkins/Loomis Agency.

Reading 3, pp. 173–175, and "Quantum Mechanics," pp. 176–177: Excerpts from Paul Fleisher, *Secrets of the Universe* (Atheneum-Macmillan Co., 1987). Reprinted by permission of Paul Fleisher and Lerner Publications. Includes three illustrations by Patricia Keeler, who has written and/or illustrated 12 books for children, from picture books to chapter books, both fiction and nonfiction. Her most recent book, *Drumbeat in Our Feet* (Lee & Low, 2006), is about Batoto Yetu, a children's African dance group.

## Chapter 8

Readings 1 and 2, pp. 186–188, 195–196: Excerpts from L. Robert Kohls, "American Values for Better or Worse," in *The Values Americans Live*, www.uri.edu.

Reading 3, pp. 203–204: Excerpt from "Hybrid-Electric Vehicles," www.ucsusa.org.